THE
OTHER
SIDE
OF THE
STREAM

THE
OTHER
SIDE
OF THE
STREAM

C.B. McCully

SWAN·HILL
PRESS

Copyright © 1998 C.B. McCully
First published in the UK in 1998
by Swan Hill Press, an imprint of Airlife Publishing Ltd

British Library Cataloguing-in-Publication Data
A catalogue record for this book
is available from the British Library

ISBN 1 84037 011 4

Typeset by Servis Filmsetting Ltd, Manchester, England
Printed in England by St Edmondsbury Press Ltd, Bury St Edmunds, Suffolk.

Swan Hill Press
an imprint of Airlife Publishing Ltd
101 Longden Road, Shrewsbury, SY3 9EB, England

To Owen Jacob –

for days past, and passing, and to come

Acknowledgements

Earlier draft versions of material that here occupies parts of chapters 4, 6 and 7 appeared in *Trout and Salmon* and the *Journal of the Grayling Society*. I am grateful to the editors of these publications for permission to reprint.

I would also like to thank Maxine Powell for her assistance in preparing successive typescripts, and to record my gratitude to Mike Davies for providing such a splendid illustrative commentary on the text.

Preface

This is not a technical book. In the first place I am incompetent to write the 'how-to' of trout fishing. In the second, fly-fishing literature is crammed with wisdom, and I would be impertinent – and dishonest – to write as if I could somehow say more about tackle, or technique. And yet. . . .

And yet over six centuries ago the anonymous author of the first fishing book in English, the *Treatise of Fishing with an Angle*, wrote that 'you shall not use this foresaid crafty disport for any covetousness to the increasing and sparing of your money only, but principally for your solace, and to cause the health of your body, and especially of your soul'. I suppose if this book is about anything, it is about that.

Chris McCully
1998

Contents

CHAPTER ONE

Becks

*I*f you drive east from York on the A166, across the flat lands bisected only by the rock fault at Garrowby Hill, and from there up onto the rolling chalk openness of the Wolds, you'll come to the market town of Driffield. This is the country of corn, the horse, and the Viking settler, a farming tenancy where the sun, seemingly just acres away, is sliced off at evening by the next fold in the land. Chalk, luminous and enriching, has given this county its character: prosperous, traditional and unspectacular. Chalk feeds the land: a handful of subsoil shows white shards of stone flaked among the loam. Chalk feeds the water: though there are few rivers, they run slow and vodka-clear, lush with weed, each one filtered by, and gathering nutrients from, unguessable tons of permeable rock. Just south of Driffield you may drive across such water, across the new bridge over the Driffield Beck.

This beck has given me some of the best and most interesting fishing of my life: two-pound browns on the floating fly, bigger (much bigger) fish risen and missed, and two specimen grayling on the artificial shrimp. I say this not so much to celebrate my own prowess, which is minimal, but to illustrate what the beck can – or could – do. I have fished here only luckily, as an infrequent if persistent guest; but the beck has treated one guest with unfailing courtesy. In every corner there have seemed to be moving trout; in every side stream the fish have risen quietly, broad-shouldered, fat and unapproachable; in each deep the grayling have shadow-haunted the stream-bed.

It is sometimes said that fishing is conscious escapism. I don't believe it. Each time I have visited the beck, there's been the same sense of waking from the world into the paradox of real enchantment.

Some spells break, and we are the spell-breakers. If you stand on the new bridge now, you will see the slow, expensive water and the trailing weed. But the fish you'll see, unless you are very lucky, will not be the wild, native trout; they'll be stock fish – heavy, no doubt, but pellet-fed and gullible. In the lower reaches, hundreds, perhaps thousands of small, voracious rainbow trout recently escaped from a nearby fish farm and filled every lie. And the grayling are listless and diseased: slowly, they seem to be disappearing. The twin evils of effluent and nitrate, the leaching-away of abstraction, and the steady encroachment of town onto country, are killing by greed. It is our greed: market forces must be served, and everything is vulnerable. The invisible stain that is souring not only Driffield but many of our waters can be traced to the money-men and the bureaucrats – and, sadly, to some fishermen as well.

Many seasons ago I walked, rod in hand, to one of the pools near Bradshaw's mill. There had been little fishing. The grayling had seemed dour and disinclined. The light had closed in early, even for December. On the carrier where I stood, the current was sluggish. A hundred yards below, where I once took thirty grayling without moving a step (returning all but three), weed unnaturally choked the stream. At my feet, a diseased grayling lay upside-down in the shallows. Its fins had a grey, luminescent tinge. Sores covered its sides and belly. As I turned the fish over with my boot I saw that tiny green leeches had fastened into the scales below the fish's once-magnificent dorsal fin. Death's scavengers were doing their work. I was about to throw the grayling up onto the bank when, very feebly, it began to kick in my hand. Feeling sick, I took out the priest and did what was necessary.

That moment marked a turning-point and a time for reassessment. Whatever the ultimate reason for that grayling's death – effluent from, ironically, a trout farm upstream, or fatal seepage from a drainage ditch, or that scourge of grayling stocks, UDN – I knew that something had gone badly wrong, and wrong not only in the ecological sense. Some malaise had struck my own fishing, and my own approach to it. It is easy to become careless and opportunist: everything is for the best in the best of all possible fishing worlds when there are fish to be caught, no matter how, no matter by whom, no matter where, nor when stocked. But the wild fish, and the streams not yet tampered with or pollution-struck, are vanishing, or perilously survive in out of the way places which haven't yet seen the dredger or the farmed rainbow or the planner's map.

Something else is vanishing, too – a sympathy, won by understanding, with fly-hatch and habitat, and a care for the future. This sympathy and care is being replaced by instant competition, by quick limits and the lure of dead fish-flesh. It is contagious, the envy of 'success', and it was this contagion with which I confronted myself over the dying grayling. And it was to find a cure, in solitude, to find joy again in the thought of fishing, that this was written.

* * * *

It's difficult to know where fishing began. In my own case there was no father or rich uncle with a rod in a nearby syndicate; there was no history of cast or creel anywhere in our family. But I think that the first bewitchment came on a small West Yorkshire beck which, for a few years at least, filled my imagination and moved my daydreams.

The beck ran into the River Aire by Myrtle Park. I fished

here, with jamjars and the obligatory string-and-pin, for summer upon summer, tethered to the bank by my mother, and caught minnows, mostly. I must have been the biggest minnow-expert in Yorkshire. And then, one summer afternoon, stirred by tales of big trout – for hadn't Geoff Scollick taken a two-pounder from the pool by the Templar's House one year? – I walked upstream, past the old pack horse bridge and the silent mill, and came out into the middle reaches that were bright with crowfoot and ringed with rising fish. I sat for hours in the grass, in the thistles and the nettles, and by the time I went home, some great readjustment had taken place at the back of my mind.

I fished the beck for the first time with a school-friend and his father. His father had a rod in the syndicate which rented the fishing-rights; these extended from the golf course up to Harden village and the Malt Shovel pub. I caught nothing, of course. Schooled on minnows and other small fry, I hadn't the faintest idea of what I was doing. Where trout would lie, or what they were supposed to eat, were mysteries as deep as Latin grammar. But Mr Booth took one fish on worm from a fast little run under the trees, and he held it out in the sunshine for me to see. He'd put it in a plastic bread bag. I took out the trout, and touched its small flanks, the rays of its fins and its bony mouth with the diamond-sharp teeth.

That, I suppose, is where my imagination was first lit by the beautiful and brilliant fish, the 'rose moles all in stipple'. From then on, I coveted them. Yet I never caught them. For a long time after I had acquired my first rod (a five-shilling cane affair with a reversible handle), and even after some omnivorous (and unsuitable) reading had taught me that trout would eat worms, and flies, too, I caught nothing. This lasted four years. Four years: two words to sum up the hopeful, self-taught ignorance between eight and twelve. Whole series of worms lay untouched in the silent pools and the jabbly runs. My mother, who had only reluctantly been persuaded that young trout-fishers should not be roped to her bankside chair, gave up asking what I had caught. As far as she was concerned, I was merely pottering a little dangerously near water, a boy lunatic in the open air.

One day, in desperation, I took off the worm and tied on a tiny spinner, and flicked it out clumsily across the big pool under the farmhouse. I had never used a spinner before – the impulse to use it was some dim equation of minnow and trout – but I made it move where I thought the fish would be lying. Halfway back into the retrieve there was a rattle on the rod. I didn't realise what had happened – with no experience behind me, how could I have done? I flicked the spinner out again, in a puzzled sort of fashion, and almost at once was plugged, terrified, into an electric fish current. (The shock which riddled my body then was not altogether unlike the one I received when I put my mother's screwdriver experimentally into an electric socket.) The five-bob cane rod bent to the butt, and, with the typical finesse of those years, I simply hung on, my knees turning rapidly to treacle. Somehow I picked up the net, an old crabbing-net pillaged from a seaside holiday, and bundled in the fish. Then I threw the whole lot up the bank, and fell on it. I was petrified. Never, I thought, would I catch a bigger trout, never again would there be such an altogether huge success. . . . Fingers shaking, I knocked the fish on the head with a stone as I had seen my friend's father do, and ran two miles upstream to his son, breathless not with running but with pride. The trout weighed just under one pound.

The capture of that one fish seemed to break the four years of zero. I caught trout then on worm, and later, on fly. Mostly I fished on my own, but later there was Robert Howard, 22 hook and 2lb line expert, and later still, Owen Jacob. Owen is one of the best fishermen I know (by which I mean one of the most thoughtful). We learned about the dry fly during hatches of spring olives, and about nymphs too. Bill Long, our staunchest and most monumentally patient family friend, gave me my first lessons in fly-tying (oddly, at the same table on which I am now writing this). And we learned about tangles and trees and wind-knots and frustration and all the rest.

In the numb winters we spent snatched Sundays home from boarding-school patrolling the beck, building ineffectual croys and clearing the banks, cutting down offending branches with a pair of secateurs.

We named the pools – mostly names taken from Plunket Greene's *Where the bright waters meet* (Deutsch: London, 1983. First edition 1924), which I had just read. There were the Beehive Bridge and the Viaduct, and others, whose names recorded the excitement of our adventures: Owen's Pool, Robert's Pool, the Camera Pool, the Farmhouse Pool, and the mysterious Monster Pool which never gave us the monster although, tantalisingly, we hooked him once. We were supremely happy, and the few years that I spent with the spring and summer olives and the willing fish were a time of experimental joy. It makes me smile now, a little sadly, to think of the dignity and importance we invested in the beck and its roll-call of named pools, some of which you could jump across and most of which you could wade in short boots.

I don't think there is a better way to learn about fishing for trout than by starting on a small beck. You learn to read water by instinct, and you learn to cast lightly and accurately and avoid drag. You have to fish upstream and keep out of sight. You have to learn about sunshine and shyness. And you learn only too well about the reactions of the fish, how one clumsy step can put down a whole poolful of moving trout, how one shadow can spoil a lie. It is an intimacy, a reciprocation, and this is a wonderful thing, for it means that to catch trout at all you must begin to think in a different dimension. This appears when you first say to yourself 'If I were a trout . . .'

My best day on the beck gave me eight fish. The biggest brace were 1lb 7oz and 1lb 6oz, both wild, and both specimens for the water. The stream was clearing and dropping after a summer spate, and the first fish came on slug, fished upstream. (The beck trout seemed to be most partial to small, dirty-white slugs. I was rather proud of my compost-heap discovery.) In the afternoon, on a clearing water, I put up the dry fly, and took the second from the same lie as I had taken the first. My diary records that the second fish was 'a real buccaneer, which tried desperately (spelt wrong) to gain the sanctuary of the wall'. It also records that the two fish 'lying in the shade of the oak tree by the pool side made a superb brace'. I hope I can be forgiven this piece of self-congratulation. It was to be another five years before I caught bigger brown trout, and these were from wider and more august waters. The little beck had done it all for me, the beginner and opportunist; the lucky.

I have said that the Harden Beck moved my daydreams. They couldn't last. By the time I was fourteen I had an arrangement with the syndicate which allowed me to fish on school holidays during the season. But the next spring, coming away from the fishing up the dusty track which led to the Twines and Bingley, I met the organiser of the fishing. He was stiff; I was tongue-tied, apart from stammering some rubbish about the Grey Duster. Looking back, I think I can see what he thought of the scruffy lad with the plastic bag full of trout swinging from his left hand. Curtly, he told me that the 'arrangement' had fallen through; I hadn't been informed. If I liked, I could fish twice more, he added, probably sensing the tears of rage and defeat that were by this time imminent. I turned from him with as much politeness as I could muster and went home, joy shattered. That night, I ruled two thick lines in my fishing diary under the last entry for Harden Beck. I never fished it again.

In front of me as I write are two diagrams, drawn on yellowed school file-paper, of 'Food Chains for Harden Beck'. At the bottom of the chain I have nominated 'Green Weed'; near the top, in suitable capitals, is the one word TROUT.

17

In between, the recipients of my haphazard arrows are nymphs, shrimps, caddis, and snails. I also mention minnows and bullheads (with which the spring trout were almost invariably gorged), and terrestrial insects (important on a small, well-bushed stream). As trout-takers I have mentioned herons, perch, rumoured otters, natural causes, rods, and poaching. In the middle of the page (and correctly spelt, by this time), I have written in pompous bold pencil that 'the food chain could, of course, be destroyed by atmospheric or aquatic pollution'.

That parenthetical 'of course'. As I shrank away from the beck, feeling chastened, so I slunk back to it not long ago. As I stood on the old bridge, where I had so often tackled up, an estate car pulled in behind me on the track. The gamekeeper, newly instituted, was keen to do his work. I assured him that my car contained nothing more harmful than a pair of waders and a piece of rope: no net; no cyanide. He eyed me suspiciously, much as I had once been eyed by the syndicate-wielder. Eventually, after some uneasy negotiation, we talked of the fishing. It was bad, he said. Pollution from a chicken farm upstream had resulted in several fish-kills. Because of the cost of litigation, not much could be done. The beck was dying.

I hope beyond hope that Harden runs bright again. I look at the schoolboy diagrams in front of me and I can see again the trout stirring in each stickle, and taste the sweat in my mouth from hot summer afternoons working a tiny dry fly under the trees, and watch a twelve-year-old boy landing his fish in a seaside crabbing-net. 'The food chain could, of course, be destroyed . . .' I haunt my own memory. Never go back.

I have begun with two becks, and should add a third, which I fished more or less at the same time as Harden. This was CrossHills Beck, which ran hard by the playing fields of my school and so marked a natural, and strictly enforced, out of bounds area. There were two good pools on the school reach, the first a classic small-stream pool with a head current that ran deeply under overhanging and exposed tree roots, the second a weir-pool, whose circulating gatherings of foam scum were constantly troubled by rising trout. These two pools were a great temptation, even under threat of cane-stripes (or worse). In my last year I fished both, darkly, secretly, and, I thought, out of sight. The method was inevitably worm, fished upstream on light tackle, although one boy, gifted with the leftovers from his grandfather's fly box, used a Greenwell, an Orange Partridge and a Dark Needle (the last two, justly famous Yorkshire wet flies), fished downstream into the slack of the weir. His efforts, and mine, were discovered immediately. The curious thing is that we suffered no dire penalty, largely because of Peter's acumen. He insisted that we should take our occasional trout to the back door of the headmaster's flat. This we did, with all due initial nervousness. The response was merely a mild 'My dear boys, well . . .' Peter is by now probably the head of an international corporation.

There are two things I remember about CrossHills. The first is the smell of wild garlic. The second is how slowly we fished. We would spend two hours over a patch of water no bigger than this table, sure that fish were there, and sure that eventually they would take. Nowadays I would fish much too quickly, covering a mile of water with fast casting and too little care, until I learned again that each pool needs a deliberate and well-planned approach, and the persistence and certainty of the young. We willed the fish to take; our hands stank of trout flesh and wild garlic, and we were happy, with delicious security in the knowledge that we were breaking the law and went unpunished. We never saw another fisherman, nor saw a dead or diseased fish anywhere on the beck within reach of the school.

It might perhaps be appropriate to give a composite account of what these small streams are like, since many people are unfamiliar with them. I don't mean that this will be a technical digression, but I should try to explain what I see when I close my eyes and imagine a North-country water. I'm not speaking now of the expensive, lush rivers such as Driffield – Yorkshire, indeed the North in general, has precious few of them – but of the rainfed streams not big enough to be called rivers, or figure in the columns of the journals. 'Rainfed' is a key word, although it can be mis-applied. Some speak of rainfed rivers and streams as if they were all acidic stickles trickling through uplands, as distinct from the more placidly flowing and yielding chalkstreams of the lowlands. But in fact there is no such easy distinction. There are rainfed streams that have a lowland character, that flow through farmland across a green, if steep, valley floor. Cattle, not sheep, graze the banks, which in places are gravelled, and in others are sandpiper-devilled clay. Where the sun strikes the watercourse through gaps in the hawthorn and alder, weed grows in the stream, to flower magnificently in the later spring. Elsewhere, a natural dam has created a less purling water, a deeper flat running below a filigree of leaves. Here it can be cool in summer, and because the trout (which are constantly rising to small specks of nothing) have time to look carefully at the artifi-cial fly, they are difficult to tempt. A little downstream, and because we are in the post-industrial North, a disused mill stands, black, echoing and vaguely urinous. A small, slabbed cut shows where the water was drawn off the fall of the stream to feed the looms, and the stream itself has backed up for a hundred yards, murmuring itself almost to sleep with tales of old trout hooked and lost, until again it is lost in the trees, beginning to meander, to lose its character as a beck before merging unspectacularly with the width of the great river of which it is the diminutive partner.

Even this is not an accurate picture of our composite (and entirely fictional) small stream. Every reach has a different flow, a different fall, a different stream-bed, and each, consequently, requires a separate approach. Here, for instance, where the beck widens across stones and gravel, is a nursery stretch that will seldom or never hold a decent trout. Here, on the other hand, where the current is squeezed almost at right-angles by a clay bank and flows under a tangle of roots and debris left by last winter's floods, here you may find trout, good trout, feeding often, although the cast needs to be accurate. Here again, the water is neither tumbling nor gravely quiet – it flows swiftly and full of light, with occasional side-reaches into deeper scours, across a boulder bed, the current separating now and then around weed trails. This is a good place to take a trout feeding on ascending nymphs, or on shrimp, although playing such a fish is difficult since the banks are low and, depending on where you cast from, there are branches above. Finally, here there is a natural fall, where the pool below is separated by two large rocks, in front of which, and to the side of which, there is always a fish lying waiting under the trickle of foam peeling from the rush. All these reaches, each pool, needs handling with a precise and separate care. Nor is there a single place where you might stand up and cast overhead. It is either creeping, or kneeling, or wading, step by ginger step. You will be side-casting forever.

The fishing should begin, surely, on All Fools' Day. April 1st is not too soon, since even in a mild and wet winter the trout will barely have recovered from spawning by then. And the streams (their anglers, too) need a resting as well as the fish. In early spring the water itself is resting, frost-cold, grey and lifeless. There's no new growth yet in or around the beck. It is the end of the dead season, the year's coma. Even now, however, and despite appearances, the natural ecology is beginning to change. The tiny trout of the winter spawning, the alevins, have lasted through the dead season on their umbilical sacs of nutrients, and now begin to feed at the edges of the streams, first on algae, then on midge larvae. As the days lengthen, the weed puts out new shoots and the spreading beds provide a haven for the increasingly numerous creatures underwater. Then, almost miraculously, the olives begin to hatch in appreciable quantities.

There's something uncanny about these first hatches. I say 'first hatches' because although I have seen grayling rising to a hatch of olives in March, it is April before the trout are really interested, moving from their winter torpor-places in the pools and beginning their prospect at the stream-heads. And it is uncanny. Around lunchtime, you see the first fly. Then another. Soon a trickle of fly is passing into the promising part of the pool, where the stream appears to thicken and drag. The trout, which have been foraging lethargically among the stones for caddis and bull-head, take up feeding positions in midwater to intercept the hatch. This is the moment. I am always just as excited as the fish, curbing (or trying to curb) my impatience to see the fly, cocked, perfect, sailing into the magic ring.

This is how it begins. After the tackle-tinkerings of the close season, after the rod-swishings in the living room (who has ever built a ceiling high enough?), after the reading of the fishing books someone bought you for Christmas, there you are – casting, hopeful, out of practice – by the awakening river, in the slow throes and cycle of another season. Later, there will be the evening fishing, perhaps (if you are cursed or lucky) the mayfly, or the stonefly. There'll be the thin days of heat and low water, the nymph, and then the sedge in the half-light, followed by the rich but unsatisfactory days of September, when you are fishing for trout against the waning of the year. Caught in this cycle, perhaps we don't realise how privileged we are, to spend days, or midge-bitten evenings, by these unsung, ungrand northern streams.

It was on these becks, mostly wadeable or jumpable, that I learned my fishing. Lured away by the siren hiss of success, it was to be years before I went back to them, after realising what folly it was to catch tailless rainbows in the dark pit-acres of the money-men. But the becks and streams survive – just – and as I went back to them, the most and least that can be said is that they welcomed me.

CHAPTER TWO
Stillwaters

*T*he pull of the unexpected, the pull of size, took me to the stillwaters. I put the becks and the bright rivers behind me (as I thought) as one would put by something embarrassing and outgrown.

Stillwater trout fishing was then, after the heady days of the 1960s and the opening of Grafham Water, rapidly developing in scope, and its adherents were vociferous, competent and, I thought, enviably successful. Of course, it is something of a falsification to speak of 'stillwater trout fishing' as if it were some undiscriminated *modus operandi*. In the first place, no water is ever still: the wind will inevitably form subsurface currents, onwashes and backwashes, and it is in these draughts of water that one will find the fish feeding. In the second place, stillwater trout fishing is nothing if not diverse. It includes the fishing on sullen ponds for quick-turnover rainbows; the more challenging fascination of the prestige waters such as Blagdon and Chew; and the altogether different experience of boatfishing on the wind-lashed expanses of the far North and West. The strategies that these three differing types of water involve are barely reconcilable. They involve different equipment, and not just a variety of flies but a variety of designs of fly. Stillwater trout fishing, therefore, by its very nature, requires a special versatility and a special kind of attention. It lends itself to experiment in a way that, arguably at least, river fishing does not. It is also, I think, a desperately exciting business – or it can be. That qualification is necessary because the spectres of cynicism and hard profit are never very far away. The black and finless rainbow, the anglers casting shoulder to shoulder, the jostling for, and staking out of, good fishing-ground – these have become far too familiar. Covetousness looks in its wallet and is there on Opening Day.

The worst examples of this kind of cynicism can be found on the tiny waters. These are sometimes mill-dams that have been converted into rainbow trout fisheries ('2 acres, open all year, best fish 18lb') by unscrupulous owners. More often they are simply purpose-built holes in the ground.

There was one near Newcastle-upon-Tyne, a dark and evil-brown-looking pit about an acre in extent near the river. The trout were kept nearby in cages, and were periodically dumped into the pit, where they could sometimes be seen swimming around the muddy margins in a dazed and disorientated manner. Some bore the tell-tale stains of disease.

On this particular pit both bait- and fly-fishing were allowed. Both were regimented. The bait-men sat lugubriously along two sides of the rectangle, while the men with the fly-rods flailed away at either end, cast after cast over the same strip of water. The bait-men favoured the use of a maggot and sweetcorn cocktail; the fly-men invariably used lures, of indescribable and luminous colours. Luminous, or at least very highly visible, lures were essential owing to the turbid oxtail-soupiness of the water. A violent shade of lime green worked best. In the shack where the tickets were sold, dog-eared photographs attested to the capture of huge, sick-looking fish.

I ask myself now why I ever fished there, amongst the mud and cigarette-butts. It was convenient, and cheap, and

I was too young, and too trout-obsessed, to realise that it is only discrimination which can foster real enjoyment and absorption.

I fished this pit twice. On the last occasion, I was told at the shack by a youth wearing a garish T-shirt that the fish were rising well. 'You'll be alright today,' he said. 'Black Pennell's the fly. There's been a good hatch of Black Pennells this week.' I bought my ticket speechlessly, looking round warily for a hatch of Baby Dolls.

The place wrote its own epitaph later that afternoon. As I was miserably and monotonously plying the rod at the far end, a rabbit bobbed out of what was left of the hedgerow just yards away, and sat on the worn-down path in the sunlight. Immediately, the youth walked up the bank with an air-gun. The rabbit sat on, so close that I could see the light reflected in its eye. The youth came nearer, raising the gun. I put down the rod, prised some loose clay from the bank, and lobbed it in the rabbit's direction. It looked round at the disturbance, but sat on. I waved my arms. The youth took aim. I opened my mouth to shout at the instant that he fired. The rabbit jerked backwards and collapsed, twitching. The youth walked round to the hedge and finished the creature off with the gun-butt.

The dispiriting thing about these places is their regimentation. It is true that they provide 'good fishing', if that phrase means competitively-priced indulgence at the expense of hungry (half-starved) rainbows and blackened, enormous brood fish. It is also true that such waters can be suitable testing-grounds for new tackle and mechanical prowess – and as such, useful for beginners, or at least, beginners like me – and that they can provide a certain kind of excitement in the play of a big trout in a narrow place. Yet this excitement and that prowess, admirable no doubt in themselves, are constrained by numbers and the clock.

On one such fishery, two-and-a-bit acres in extent, a whistle blows at 8 a.m. to signal the start of the 8–12 shift.

The same whistle sounds at 12 noon, and at 4 p.m., at which times the incoming anglers stand in the outgoing anglers' bootprints, hauling away over the same 2,500 fish. This fishery (whole pints of Pennine bitter would not make me reveal its name) is by no means atypical. And again, cynicism is rife. Fishing the early shift, for example, while the motor of the aerator hummed fifty yards away, I had worked hard to locate, at depth, some decent, possibly overwintered rainbows. I caught one on a small black Muddler, worked slowly back to me on a sinking line. As I was netting the fish, the owner of the water loomed behind me. 'Nice fish,' he said. 'What d'you get it on?' I slipped the hook out of the fish's jaw and held up the little Muddler. 'Ah,' he said, 'looks just like a pellet, dunnit?'

Now I happened to know, admittedly more by luck and persistence than by delicate judgement, that there was a group of fish twenty yards in front of me feeding in mid-water on black pupae. The little Muddler on the sinking line had been chosen because the two would fish at an appropriate depth; and the Muddler, in small sizes at least, is a useful caricature of the natural fly. I actually thought, in my innocence, that I had been fairly clever. But, 'looks just like a pellet, dunnit?'. Perhaps I'm too fastidious, but I fished half-apologetically until the lunchtime whistle, and felt guilty for the rest of the day.

Ultimately, I think that these small fisheries have little to do with fly-fishing as I conceive it. Here it is, then, that I must risk a definition. Fly-fishing is:

> the intent to capture wild or naturalised game fish on an artificial fly designed to simulate some food item which those fish might be expected to see and eat (or to have seen and eaten) in the normal course of events and in the appropriate places.

It is a long definition, a long sentence full of complicated matter, of half-evasions and trouble, but it is as close to the difficult truth as I can get. What does such a definition

26

include? Wild browns, yes, on appropriate representations, which last must surely include the great traditional patterns; naturalised rainbows, too – the difficult fish, stocked for weeks or months, which imperturbably cruise the surface film on calm summer evenings and are hair-tearingly uncatchable; and sea trout, pulsebeat-inducing and mysterious, tails whirring through their leap in the mid-summer darkness, or pluming near the boat out of the bitter peat emptinesses in the far West; and finally, I include without any apology those shadow haunters of the stream-bed, the grayling. All these I include, but not the salmon, an altogether different and more expensive creature of which I have had little personal experience (I have caught a bare half dozen, always by accident), and thus arbitrarily exclude. And the flies; what flies does that definition include? Teams of buzzers; the floating olive or sedge; terrestrials; pinfry; shrimps and hoglice; the sparse-set drift of three northern wet flies fished across in spring; and the wake of a heavy-hackled bobfly cutting the surface in a good blow. All these flies, and the styles of presentation their fishing involves, are properly representative. This is a key word, and we could even claim that in this sense fly-fishing is like every art: it cannot exactly imitate, but it can and must represent. We might, indeed we should, come back to this later. For the present, however, that definition will have to serve. It includes all the interest and joy and absorption I need, and it excludes the pellet-Muddler and the good hatch of Black Pennells. So be it.

* * * *

I need to go back to the lakes, in folly and tribute. Where did I first learn about lakes? The answer comes back like a remote echo: Cashel and the West – a place at the back of my mind where the wind hurls itself at Ireland from the Atlantic, where the rivers are turbulent or lily-calm in turn, and where the lakes, properly loughs, are glacial chains, systems of light set in a vast peat bog. Just the names are an incantation of great happiness: Ballynahinch, Gowla, Inver, Cashla, Screeb. And the lough names: Annilaun, Invermor, Ahalia, Rusheen, and always Cureel, its two syllables of light, liquid sound invoking a faded Instamatic picture of two minor-public-schoolboys, one of whom is holding a 4lb white trout and has just become a legend, while the other is wearing a ridiculous hat.

These boys are Owen and I. Owen figured earlier as one of the best fishermen I know. I think so now; it says something about our long understanding that I thought so then, when in our early years, part-boys, part-men, we fished the waters of the West together, our heads full of fishing, and space, and all the future.

The fishing was spectacular, and quite different from anything I had known. I had never fished for sea trout (white trout) before; nor had I ever been in a boat before apart from one or two stern afternoon exercises with my sisters on Cartwright Lake in Bradford. The demands white trout fishing makes on even a young brain are quite different from the demands made by beck brown trout. On the becks, you have to think in terms of natural food, of lies under stones and of seasonal hatches. On the loughs, you think in terms of water, the rain that has fallen in the night, the height of the river, the light, and above all the wind. Fishing for brown trout on rivers requires a specific kind of concentration; you attack the fish intensively. Fishing on the lough, however, requires a generalised concentration, taking many variables (water, light, wind) into account – the fish are thus approached extensively. White trout also hardly feed in freshwater. You cannot really present them with a pattern that is a representation of what they are actually eating at that moment. You must approach them with a pattern that stimulates or engages their memory or their temporary caprice. Even then, white trout fishing is no stimulus-and-response, Pavlovian experiment. For most of the time, you know that your approach will be at least partly wrong. Paradoxically, this mystery is also totally captivating, largely because fishing for white trout cannot be carried out by hard logic. Hard logic is used for a chalkstream trout feeding on Pale Wateries in a difficult place, or for a big lake brown trout feeding to pinfry on a regular beat; these are the opportunities for reason and empiricism. But white trout fishing is not rational in this sense (certainly not in Ireland); it is mostly imagination. Think of it, of all the variables: the last flood, then the fish settling into the lough. Where? Then the light: too bright? Or a good dull stun on the wavetops? Then the wind: unsettled and gloomy squalls from the west, or a steady blow, or a calm in which it's difficult if not impossible to present a fly? Then back to the fish: how long have they been in the lough? Are they mainly herling, or did a run of bigger fish get up last week? All these questions. And then, even then, when you have weighed all this up, selected flies, tried likely drifts, still the fish won't take. Why? Why? And yet Owen, who is fishing just the same flies, at the same speed, at the same depth, only from the other end of the boat, Owen has four, and good fish too. Mystery and imagination: his mind is full of fish running unseen from the sea, of the weight of lough water on stones in age-old lies, of the falling river, of the soft day and the soft light. He is thinking trout.

Now let me explain that faded Instamatic photograph. Cureel is one of the loughs on the Inver system, remote for men, and hard to reach even for fish, since there's a barrier fall below it which is impassable to white trout except in a big flood. A big flood in the West means three days and nights of rain after a dry spell – rain looming in purple clouds over the Twelve Pins, then driving horizontally, fretting the bog-cotton, laying the dust on the road in rivulets, before gathering all air with it and passing into the Maam Turks with a continual soft hiss of dark, misty downpour. After three days and nights of this, and the wind thrashing the firs around the house restlessly, you can begin to think of fishing Cureel.

Extraordinary things happened to us on this lough. The year we first fished it together (we were both fourteen) we had six fish weighing just over six pounds – an unremarkable statistic. Yet Owen's first fish wasn't caught so much as entangled. The hook had come free during the play, but by that time the line was so wound round the fish's body that it was easy to net the poor creature. Our second fish was my first lough white trout, and at just under 2lb, a shock to the system. I was trembling so much with terrified excitement that I had to stop fishing for several drifts, and simply looked at the fish laid out on the bow thwart: the adoration of the trout. Later that evening, Owen took what was up to that time his best ever fish from Connemara. It was a strange and beguiling day.

All that autumn, and into the next school year, we ached to get back. I still have Owen's exquisite line-drawings of the flies we were to take: Kingsmill-Moore's Claret Bumble, a small Watson's, and the Daddy. We used to talk quietly about these patterns at the back of the class during biology lessons, where we also, regrettably, sketched likely drifts onto quarto file-paper and read back-issues of *Trout and Salmon* under the table. Biology lessons were, we felt, a proper environment for this sort of activity. The fact that we both subsequently passed the exam is a tribute to Irish white trout and an exceedingly tolerant teacher.

The next year we walked out to Cureel again over the half-made track from Luggeen. In retrospect it seems as if the hotel – the Zetland ran all the fishing – outdid itself in kindness in allowing us to fish such good loughs (and so cheaply) during the best part of the season, and in truth Sean Nixon, the fishery manager, seemed to have a benevolent eye on us. A big man, all-controlling, standing among fishing rods and over the massive ledger that held all the fishing returns since the early part of the century, he was our source and runestone. That morning, and with a knowing smile, he spoke the word we had waited a year to hear: Cureel.

The day began in a flat calm. Midges rose and fell in murmurous columns in the luxuriant vegetation of Cureel's islands. Horseflies crawled across the blue boat-wood, bloated and troublesome. We discussed flies and tactics desultorily, biology-lesson hope gone. The Daddy dangled uselessly from the rod tip. Two Watson's were hooked, dry and pristine, into the corks. We began to eat lunch: flat Club orange, cheese sandwiches that had peeled in the heat, and apples that tasted sour.

Then came cloud, and with the cloud, the wind. Lunch was abandoned. The first fish was in the boat not long after, another Cureel unfortunate that had actually shed the hook in the water at the lee of the boat before Owen moved speedily with the net. In those days I couldn't recognise the ethical problem this posed, and fished on, intent. Owen next took two herling, bright, rod-bending little fish. The lough was coming alive.

As soon as the lough lived, it died. This is a curious feature of white trout fishing in the West. There are almost invariably two taking periods in the day, periods when the fish are active, poised near the surface or swimming about in small shoals. The first period lasts from mid-morning until lunchtime, an Irish lunchtime, which can be anywhere from 11.30 until 3 in the afternoon; the second period comes in the early evening. At least, this is the pattern on the loughs, and the spells of fish activity there may possibly be related to the fishes' feeding activity in the sea. We wished, year on year, for a taking period that would extend right through the day, and we would bring such fishes back. It never came.

And so Cureel died on us, as we half-expected. We tried drift on mechanical drift, working up the lough to the river mouth. Then Owen changed fly, putting up an obscure, and very brightly-coloured pattern called, I think, the Raymond. Colman Nee, one of the Zetland's gillies, swore by it, but it was an unlikely-looking specimen. Most Connemara white trout flies are sober, indeed, tweed-mixes of black or claret, with nothing to relieve the mix but perhaps a small touch of red somewhere and a hint of silver twist showing through the dubbing. The Raymond, on the other hand, is a streamlined fragment of tinsel and colour, with a married wing of yellow, aquamarine and violent red. It is as if one glimpse of a kingfisher, an electric blue bolt among yellow iris, has been imagined onto a hook. This fly Owen put up, middle dropper.

Two or three drifts later, when the leader was no more than twelve feet from the boat, he raised the rod; and the rod pulled over. Ten minutes afterwards, ten minutes when our hearts nearly stopped beating, a 4lb white trout lay on the boards. It had taken the Raymond.

A 4lb white trout is not a big fish by English standards, but it is big for the West, and enormous to two fifteen-year-olds. I don't think there are many fish of this weight caught in Connemara each year – certainly not now – and many fishermen there judge a 2lb white trout as a good one. And so the photograph was taken; and so we slapped each other on the back and shook hands and swore; and so Owen became a legend that day, turning home with the dead weight of fish on his back and his eyes full of scales, and was happy.

There are two footnotes to this story. Although we caught other fish that day, and the catch was a good one, of course it is the 4lb trout that we remember. But it was the only fish to take during the dead spell of the afternoon and it was the only fish to take the Raymond. Riddle me that; but riddle it how you will, what that fish means is mystery and imagination. No law or logic governed its capture, only one fisherman following a hunch that was more than a hunch. Only the very best fishermen, speculative and empathetic, have this gift.

The second footnote is less savoury, but tells me that even as we walked back down the road to Cashel ('with steam coming out of your ears,' as Owen's mother reminded me recently) another world was waiting for us, full of much smaller things, of jealousies, disappointments and worry.

The custom at the Zetland was for each boat to return to the back bar and lay out their catch on the fish-slab there. This we duly did, still lit by excitement and pride. The news travelled fast to the hotel's paying customers over their pre-dinner gins and tonic. We both told the story several times over the fish-slab. Then one sneering individual put his well-ginned face up to Owen's, took one look at the catch, and spat 'Beginners' luck' before disappearing again in the direction of dinner. Although he left an appalled silence behind him, I have loathed the man for twenty and more years, and I'm afraid I loathe him still. The only satisfaction I can feel is that I know he will be a beginner all his life.

Cashel and the West, where I first began to learn about the lake, the techniques of the slow draw and the long lift, the deadliness of the dibble and the brute facts of boat-handling. But we have gone from the ridiculous, the acre pit and its empty rainbows, to the sublime, or nearly sublime. What of the other stillwaters? Let me take you to one, full of wild or almost wild brown trout that are difficult.

'Difficult' is, as anyone who has fished for more than one or two seasons knows, a relative term. On occasions, this lake (a North-country tarn) can yield its fish with a thrawn generosity, but mostly you or I would do well to take a brace apiece. Yet the fish are big: the lake lies on limestone, and its ecology is rich. A three-foot carpet of pondweed fronds the lake-bed, full of shrimps and snails and hoglice. In the stones, there are caddis. Everywhere there are the ubiquitous buzzers; on a calm, rain-stopped evening in late spring the air will be black with them. As if this richness were not enough, in summer the tarn teems with trans-lucent needles of perch-fry in millions.

Some Julys ago, together with an exceptionally skilled friend, I rowed out from the boathouse into a virtually unfishable gale. Gales pursue me when I fish (so, inciden-tally, do flat calms, sometimes on the same day). But this was no ordinary gale. It brought driving rain and lost the surrounding hills. The lake hissed venomously in a stinging mist. Soon, the bottom of the boat was awash, and we thought hard about a short row back to the boathouse and the comfort of a slow hour or two with the hipflasks. At that moment, Mark's rod went up and the gale howled on the line, now taut with a trout. We were able to see little of the ensuing fight – to look upwind was to be needle-lashed by the storm – but eventually the fish, a good one of about 1½lb which had taken a small silver-bodied wet fly, came to the net. We could see almost nothing except a circle of wind-harried lake immediately around the boat; elsewhere, the world had disappeared into rain. It felt as if we had taken a trout from among clouds.

An hour later it was my turn to hook a fish just under 2lb close to the shore, where white horses were combing over pale rock. Again the trout had taken a silver fly (a Silver Invicta) and was stuffed, like the first, with pin-fry. We went in to have lunch and to dry off, and laid the fish out, hand-heavy and well-marked, on the stone dock. A brace of fish by lunchtime is satisfying; the two are tokens of hard work and hope. My mind ran with epigrams, and promising clichés like 'big wave, big fish'. As we rowed out again into the clearing afternoon, I said to Mark that we could expect anything.

The afternoon was a classic of rolling waves and taking trout. The gale passed away gloomily to the north, leaving behind it a steady blow, good for drifting. Some fish came, as we expected, to pin-fry patterns like the excellent Silver Invicta, whose touch of blue jay stylises the watery aquamarine tint that you see when the light catches the flank of the natural fry. Other trout, more curious than determined, would follow the dibble, taking the fly (or missing it) from a long, slanted approach across the comber tops. The fish were restless and eager, and big. We caught nothing under 1½lb – large for wild fish – and they were full-scaled, full-finned, full of energy and perfectly proportioned.

Towards the early evening we moved to another part of the lake, an area of shallows over which the gulls were working, picking up pin-fry with a clumsy but effective splash and a raucous wail of success. We had barely started the new drift when there was a quick brown movement to the Silver Invicta. I felt the hook bite, then a brief agony of lost contact. Then the rod bucked down again and the fish was on solidly.

It was bigger, much bigger. The backing was showing on the reel spindle before I realised that I could barely hold this trout. 'Mark, I can't stop it,' I said.

He was already on the oars, following the fish into the lake. The reel was still yelling; a red welt was forming on my left palm where I had tried, ineptly, to brake the drum. 'You'll have to stop it,' he said, unanswerably.

I felt numb and disastrous. Out in the lake, there was a boiling thrash from an enormous trout. 'Christ,' I thought, then suddenly knew that that fish was my fish, which had leaped, turned, and was now running back towards the boat with only the dead pull of waterlogged line on the rod. I reeled with hopeless ecstasy, and was aware of irrelevant things – the dull creak of the oars, the wind's blunt noise in my ears, a curlew weeping in the sky overhead. Then I regained direct contact, but not for long before the fish repeated its first performance.

Halfway through the play I realised that something was wrong, and my heart sank. 'Mark, it's foulhooked.' Everything pointed to it; that moment of lost contact when the fish had taken; the unstoppable wild rushes; the fact that I was powerless to turn the trout's head; and now, in the later stages, the fact that I was incapable of working the fish back to the boat. I felt an overwhelming disappointment.

The fish wallowed ten yards upwind. We could see the fly, the Silver Invicta, precariously stitched into the trout's flank just above a pectoral fin. The trout was now heavily spent, with no strength to run. On the other hand, there was neither the power in the rod, nor the security in the hook-hold, to risk bullying the fish over the waves to the net. The fish continued to wallow; the rod continued to bend. Stalemate. Eventually, with a judicious bit of boatmanship from Mark and some brute force from the rod-butt, the fish came close enough.

My first thought was of size; my second was of release. We both knew, and said to each other, that this was what we had to do. The fish was too big, too beautiful and too unlucky to be killed.

We tried. We tried holding the fish in the net; tried holding its head upwind; tried rubbing our hands along its body, as if, absurdly, we could have stroked it back to life. None of it was any good. The trout was half dead, its gills flooded and its body inert. The priest finished it. It weighed a mere touch under 4lb.

I have that weight on my conscience as I write, and think back to all the other fish, the hundreds taken, the fish hooked and lost, those Irish unfortunates, the lough trout, the beck trout, and I can see the stones, or the clinkers in many boats, stained with blood.

Mixed up in this is another image: a rabbit gun-butted to death. Yes, lake fishing can be a desperately exciting business, but I am disturbed now by its epics of tarnished pride.

CHAPTER THREE
Death of an Entomologist

I have come too far. It is too soon to analyse tarnished pride, although of course it is that faded effigy, hope, and with it innocence, that hangs in my mind as I write. All that joy – a tanned, unlined face burning in the wind. It surprises me, how much we lose, and how much must forget. Perhaps we too are condemned, can never run to peace, our minds full of worry; and the continual sense of being sorry.

It's not just writing and remembering that bring us to our lost roads and all our wrong turnings. The face of a boy playing his first trout confronts us just as well, and can make us realise the hugeness of the love we have failed to keep. But then, that's just it; we must forget. As this happens, as our minds empty themselves of that securing light where trout will always rise, empty themselves of becks and bright waters, then they are filled in turn with diaries, marriages, telephones, hospitals. The whole paraphernalia of the adult is sucked into the space that was once a boy. Beyond that, there are only the persistent

37

silences and griefs as the best friends you have known lose contact and become loaded with doctors, pills, divorces, silence. This, also, must be so. And we must go on.

From Connemara to the North-country and the last big trout took childhood away. The face which landed that foul-hooked four-pounder had lines, could swear thoroughly, belonged to work, responsibilities; it had known unhappiness. Naturally, there had been fishing in between, but it took years before I could recognise a trout feeding to pin-fry, could watch black midges and find them promising, could say Olive Upright and match the phrase with the fly.

During this period, I became polysyllabic. Unfortunately, I became that pomposity, a purist. I became at least something of an entomologist.

It is true that Owen and I were happy in the West's vivid years; but it's also true that, in a sense, the West taught us too well. To step into any boat thereafter brought some kind of instinctive reaction, at least to me (Owen, typically, was less affected), which meant a nine or ten-foot rod, a ten-foot leader, 6lb line, and three traditional wet flies. That was boat fishing, inscribed in books, legitimised by time. My single flybox, once decorated with general-purpose olive copies and Yorkshire spiders, was now full of Bibios, Bumbles, and the colour black. I kept favourite casts coiled neatly on old Christmas cards, the flies hooked into flimsy paper, neatly labelled. Wherever the rod was put up, the relevant pre-constructed cast would be exhumed, tied on, and fished; and fished. My battered, sparsely-furnished, much-used set of tackle; and its single flybox.

It's also true that I caught trout. Over the gulf of memory, energy and knowledge that separates the boy from this writing hand with whisky glass, I envy and admire my own simplicity.

Some short time ago I took a boat with my solicitor. We were down to fish a good Midlands stillwater, and the April day looked promising. Fish would come to lures early on, then we would move over the deep water by the dam, and pick up fish cruising on midges. At some point we would take lunch; at several points we would take photographs. A thorough and professional plan, fitting for thorough and professional men.

We took four rods into the boat, already made up; half a dozen flyboxes; lunches – monumental lunches – in plastic bags; beer; boat seats; flasks; expensive camera equipment (none of which I knew how to work); towels, two; basses, two; drogues, two; nets, two. Most of this equipment, to my shame, was mine. The whole paraphernalia of the adult. We took (rather, David took) one fish, although the wind, the light, the midges and the rise were right. I would have backed the boy, the boy with the mangled sandwiches and the box full of black flies, to have taken half a dozen.

Sometimes the luck goes, and with it, the confidence. This is a very curious thing, and one for which I have no explanation, although, God knows, I have thought about it enough. But maybe it's like the image of a boy, his head full of trout and the love of fish and fishing. As that love is leached away, or vanishes into its pale apology, sentiment, then it is replaced by the jabbering clutter of adult life. And perhaps, just perhaps, what happens when our fishing luck vanishes is similar. We replace our luck with clutter: we tie hundreds of flies; buy a new net; new rods; different densities of line that we have been gullible enough to think will purchase trout. When luck runs out it is very like unhappiness, to be bought off metaphorically in a frenzy of hard work, or bought off literally by an afternoon in the city with a credit card. It is possible that the measure of our marriages is made up of new clothes.

And so I come back to my tackle and its heap of ordered chaos, and specifically, to the flyboxes, that have grown from one to six and more. They reproach me for my lack of skill, and lack of luck. It is a strange thing, to think that at seventeen, with my three flies, ten-foot cast, floating line and unsuitable rod, I would have stepped into any boat and onto any river bank feeling big with opportunity and success.

Where ignorance is bliss, it is certainly folly to be wise. Yet I chose folly, principally because I loved the books. The word *entomology* gave me a hot shock. The Latin tags – *Cloëon dipterum, Baëtis rhodani* – were a satisfactorily impressive novelty. And the pictures: an aristocracy of olives; a scuttling clergy of sedges in their cowls; that third, rain-fed estate, the stoneflies; and then the jobbing labourers, black gnats, terrestrials, ants and smuts. These comprised, and still in many cases do comprise, the covert ranking of entomological handbooks. I would quibble with that ranking now. But then, avid amateur with a mind full of wings and names, I believed everything. Anyone sensible would have seen that I was 'Going through a phase'. My mother probably did; but at the time, I would have sold her to be called Purist. I broke out into a microscope, a magnifying glass, tweeds, and a set of appalling cravats.

The change is very marked in my fishing diaries. Of course, I had acquired some limited entomological knowledge over the years – had learned to recognise the commonest olive duns and spinners, could distinguish a trout feeding to hatching nymphs in a turbulent stickle – but this was indeed strictly limited knowledge. In particular, I knew nothing about the fly-life of lakes. In 1977, for instance, I had the luck to fish a private loch in Galloway. The fish were rising; it was mid-June, and midgy. The diary records that 'all through the day the trout were showing – porpoising on the surface as they fed on nymphs just below the surface film'. In a later entry, for the same day, I have written 'chironomids (?)'.

I fished that day, with the trout-porpoises rising all round the boat to midges – something I had at least a dim suspicion of – with three flies: a Zulu, a Wickham's, and a Butcher. It was an entirely typical piece of haphazard. Not that this approach was, or is, altogether wrong; but it was unsystematic, and in those times, system was what I began to crave.

Three years later, my diary has broken out into Latin tags such as *Chironomus anthracinus* and *Endochironomus albipennis*. The Cove PTN was a much-used fly of the time, along with various designs of hatching midge and sedge (*Limnephilus lunatus, Hydropsyche pellucidula* . . .). The principal reason for this shift of emphasis was the fishing at Coldingham Loch, and Brian Clarke's *Pursuit of stillwater trout* (London: Deutsch. 1975).

Coldingham, tucked away on the far north-east coast, is a benevolent oddity of a water. When the east wind blows, and the cold haar settles over the headland, its 27 acres almost disappear into a troutless, milky-grey light. It is prey to sudden fits of sun and flat calm, hot afternoons where damsels tick in the air, when you can smell the mud drying out underfoot, when the brightness is enough to split the stones. In the spring, your hands can cramp so badly with the cold that it's almost impossible to tie on a fly. Yet, in this changeable, important place, lessons could be learned.

Of course I had seen Brian Clarke's work serialised in that continuing authority, *Trout and Salmon*, during the mid-1970s (Owen and I had analysed the articles in whispers at the back of those biology classes), but few were the opportunities to put his insights into practice. Then came Coldingham, a belated purchase of the full text with its luminous cover full of swirling rainbow, and the realisation that I too, along with thousands of others averaging 1.7 of a sawn-off trout per outing, had shared his quest – for system, for some viable, almost empirical procedure with which to conjure trout from stillwater disturbed by the whorls of rising fish.

It happened just as the book said it should. As the warm April afternoon gave way to a cool breeze from the north, and evening, the trout of Coldingham began to rise. I see them now in my mind's eye as it clears; a ring, another ring, and then an excited splash as some frenetic rainbow turns on pupae subsurface. I hear the fish; below the breeze, and above the muttering from a boat on the other side of the

loch, the trout start moving in that aural threshold, whor-
ling, water-shifting, once, twice. . . . I turn my head to the
sound of the last rise, and see the ripples ebbing, fading,
dying away altogether into the last light.

It was the first time I had fished specifically with midge
patterns. I had come, I had seen, and recognised. There
was no flailing away with a Mallard and Claret and a
Wickham's, only a calm, reasoned, finger-fumbling attempt
to tie on the black midge artificials as the rise began.

The line lies straight across the ripple, and I'm watching
the leader butt, or watching the end of the line, feeling the
bow of line at the end of the rod tip weigh in my hands,
waiting for fish, fish which must have already seen my two
flies. *Chironomus* . . . *anthracinus* . . . or is it *plumosus?*
Perhaps it's too early in the year for *plumosus*. The truth is,
I don't know. Watch . . . the. . . . And now I'm inching back
the flies in tiny pulls, coiling the line into my left hand, the
glib slipperiness under my fingers. Watch . . . the. . . . And I
realise that I am doing something extraordinary, something
entirely new, something 'imitative'. For the first time, I'm
thinking like a fish, presenting the flies with a kind of sub-
aqueous empathy, with something like imagination.

There's another fish. Hell, they're rising well. I'm sure the
midges are big and black; I saw some in the cobwebs
under the boathouse gutters. The pupae. . . . Another cast.
The wind's dying. I can feel the evening on my cheek.
There are hundreds of buzzer shucks in the water here, just
look. And concentrate. Watch . . . the. . . . How do people
see the end of the leader at twenty yards? I can't. Inch back
the flies again, a slow sympathy. Still watching. . . . Another
fish, and. . . .

Suddenly the line weighs, goes away, across the ripple,
and in response the rod goes up, bucks, takes the kick and
run of the first trout. As I work him closer, darkly swirling, I
see that he's a brown . . . taking off again as he sees the net,
and me. And then he's in the net, bowed, and I lift him in
the mesh and take out the priest, feeling pleased, although

this is the part of the business I like least. Still, I knock him on the head, quickly, three taps, and then, because I am now a Purist, I take out the marrow spoon feeling self-conscious. It's a great moment. As Brian Clarke had said, 'my first fish on a "natural food" fly' – at least on stillwater. I saw the fish feeding to midges; offered them midge patterns; caught them on midge patterns. . . . I twist and withdraw the marrow spoon. The brown trout is full of snails.

Coldingham taught me much. Later in those summers, we caught fish which, in autopsy, proved to have been taking midges at the precise moment of hatching ('eclosion', I would then have said knowingly), and designed patterns with hackle-fibre or marabou shucks. We fished sedges into the darkness. During hot spells, or when the fish were down, we experimented with deeply-sunk hoglice fished on 20-foot leaders, daydreaming in the heat – until the fish took, hooking themselves with an angry ferocity, sullen, in the deepest parts of the loch. But most of all, it's the midges I remember: *anthracinus*, *plumosus*, the Campto midge, hooked profiles, sprightly, on the surface. We were midge sophisticates. My flyboxes broke out smugly into neat rows of olive, red, and black, dusted with white where I had tied in filamentous breathers.

I say 'we caught', 'we fished', 'we were'. It was one of the joys of those brief years that, almost for the first time, I was fishing with a group of men whose passion was trout: Don Gibson, who could catch trout from roadside puddles; Matt Bentley, zoologist, darts-player, powerful at pints; Charles Storey, historian, traditionalist, keen-eyed; Andy Gould, whose cut-glass voice I hear now under its officer's moustache ('Hello cheps. Bladdy hell'); Howard Seabrook, gentle and unconvinced, who loved trout fishing but was equally happy catching pinkeens on a roach pole in some semi-stagnant, verdant lowland pool where nothing moved except the haze; and Graham MacGregor, whose excellence as a linguist was only surpassed by his curiosity about, and enthusiasm for, catching fish. They were splendid men. But, as ever, *ubi sunt?* We have declined into mis-understandings and sporadic Christmas cards, living busily in our raw towns, successful and plausible. But Coldingham remains, and perhaps carries a trace of us still, some stain on the air where we were once happy, or, very faintly echoing as the suns sets redly behind the firs and night comes on, the sound of voices from around the far side of the loch where Don, and all the others, have been catching fish on (what else?) the hatching midge.

At about the same time, I was learning more about the entomology of rivers, and again, the change in the fishing diaries is most marked. In 1977 I knew a little – about olives, stoneflies and caddis – but it was an indiscriminate knowledge, and typically I would fish three wet flies down-stream (Orange Partridge, Dark Needle, Waterhen Bloa) or 'a good general pattern' upstream, dry (Greenwell's, Imperial). But the time had come when I had to acquire a finer recognition. The rage for order and system steamed gently under my tweeds; the appalling cravats purpled with excitement at names like *Centroptilum luteolum*, *Ephemerella ignita*, and *Rhithrogena semicolorata*. I set off with my magnifying glass and collecting bottle, poking around lumberingly under stones from Caithness to Cornwall, pulling out hanks of weed, myopically counting tails, femur sections, costal projections. And yes, the time did come when I could say to myself 'Mmm. Very nice specimen of *Ecdyonurus dispar*', although that time was not far distant from the day when, embarrassingly, I failed to recognise a mayfly (*Ephemera danica*). A mayfly, for heaven's sake – the biggest, most easily identifiable fly that floats. I even drew it in my diary, and alongside it wrote 'What's this?' I was blinded by science, perhaps, or refer-ence books. Maybe I had confused it with a large brook dun (female – *Ecdyonurus torrentis*) or a yellow may dun (male – *Heptagenia sulphurea*). It was folly to be wise, and my head was full of folly. As I got down suitably on one knee to cast suitably to a suitable trout (upstream dry, of course), feeding to, say, *Procloëon pseudorufulum*, my mind clanged weightily with Latin. I was heavy with the scrap metal of nomenclature. I am surprised now that the kneeling *poseur* didn't keel over with the weight and lie on the bank twitching.

I ask myself now whether any of this made me a better fisherman. The answer is, has to be, no. Not for the first time, I was going about things the wrong way. Many of the insects I short-sightedly murmured over occurred either rarely or not at all in the rivers I habitually fished. Other insects, painstakingly collected, were seldom eaten by the trout, which preferred caddis and bullhead to dear old *Ecdyonurus dispar*. Nor do I think that the trout greatly care whether the insect they are about to eat is the male or female of its species. Finally, the entomological handbooks seemed to concentrate very heavily on the upwinged files – a legacy of Halfordiana. Yet, in the rivers I fished, and still fish, I find the vast majority of the trout I catch have been feeding on other insects ('little black jobs', as one friend calls them), caddis, crustaceans, or small fish. There are exceptions to this, of course – last season I came back from a delightful day on the Wharfe where fish took Large Dark Olives all morning, and Iron Blues all afternoon – but they are not so many as the reference books might lead us to believe. Above all, I suppose I made the mistake of thinking that all trout were epicures. Perhaps they are, on southern chalkstreams. But on my unsung waters they were, and are, trenchermen, stone-guzzlers, greedy, and sometimes, rather stupid. After all, while it is true, as J.R. Harris claimed, that those who only use 'a good copy of general fly' may be missing out on much of the intellectual excitement fly-fishing has to offer, it is also true on perhaps seven occasions out of ten that that 'good copy of general fly' is quite as effective as the most accurate and microscopically-detailed imitation. I would rather go fishing with a Black and Peacock Spider, or Halford's despised Hare's Ear, than spend time wrecking my eyes on a parachute-hackled, upside-down-and-almost-exact copy of this week's variety of *Procloëon rufulum* – a copy which I could hardly bear to put up and get wet.

So I come back again to my tackle, and to the flyboxes. I peer into them, and find that entomology has given way to pragmatics. I no longer (that is, I rarely) tie up patterns I will never use. 'Imitation' has given way to silhouette and a sense of overall structure. I have returned, or tried to return, to a new simplicity. I no longer think in terms of individual pattern, rather in terms of groups (upwinged flies, sedges, midges, fry and other small fish, shrimps and hoglice). Happily, I have forgotten my Latin, and the entomologist collapsed in wreaths of polysyllables years ago. Filling his tweeds is someone who prefers to think more practically: What sort of fly is it? How is that trout seeing the fly? Is it taking the fly on, or in, or under the surface? For this chap, the central problem is not how to 'imitate', but how to *represent*. But for all that, I still have far too many flies, six boxes and more full. They are precious.

One box holds mayflies and Daddies, another the usual dry standards hooked into the foam in no particular order and with higgledy-piggledy hackles. A third box, a little Wheatley which has been with me for twenty years, holds buzzers, one row of which were the first flies I tied at school and which I have never been able to bring myself to part with even though the hooks are rusty. A fourth box holds Yorkshire wet flies on one leaf, shrimps, bugs and leaded nymphs on another, Irish and Scottish boat-fishing (sea trout) patterns on another, with general sedge and midge point and dropper flies on the last leaf (the leaf that includes Drunken Experiments and Disasters). A fifth wallet contains lures, sea trout flies, and a handful of salmon flies looking out of place. A sixth box, donated by someone I used to know, is empty: I leave flies to dry in it. The general impression of the collection is of an entomological jumble-sale: there are too many flies, sometimes too many of just one pattern (ten copies of one particular

Olive, a fly which caused me much vexation some years ago at Driffield); they appear to be in no particular groupings, although here and there efforts have been made to put sedge with sedge, nymph with nymph, dry with dry, and leaded with leaded. But these efforts at tidiness have hardly been successful. In fact the only time my flyboxes ever look respectable is towards the beginning of a new season. Each fishing trip thereafter seems to bring increasing chaos: leaded Shrimps jostle for position with dry Ants; Bibios jockey with Appetizers; nymphs are intermingled with Daddies. Several of the flies bear tell-tale strands of nylon, still knotted in at the eye: another evening-rise gone wrong. Yet, for all the mess and catholicism, I see the simplicity I am looking for.

In the beginning, I didn't seek simplicity: simplicity was thrust upon me. Bill Long patiently taught me to tie flies at the kitchen table, on an old-fashioned spike-vice intended for a more leisurely era when fishermen walked to the water's edge, plucked a handful of sheep's wool from the fence, stuck the vice into the earth, and sat down to tie the fly they would be fishing with ten minutes later. We fitted our vice into another vice, Heath Robinson-style, and tied Orange Partridges. Those thumb-swithering, fibre-fankling, finger-defying Orange Partridges: it took weeks just to learn to tie in the silk. Neat bodies, with the silk wound in abutting turns down to the tail and then up again, were beyond me (there were no bobbin-holders in those days). Hackles were horrors of wisps and unwindings. The preparation of the hackle was the worst part; stripping off the fluffy stuff on the flue, then parting the medial fibres between wetted forefinger and thumb so that they formed a pair of 'wings' on either side of the stalk, then moistening the very tip of the hackle. A properly-prepared feather would fall when dropped in a single plane, and not spin or twist. At least, that was the idea. Bill could do it every time; my feathers spun like sycamore seeds. Eventually, I learned the knack, and some sort of hackle would be twisted on.

Typically, this operation would leave no room for the head of the fly. I think I grew up believing that the eye of a hook was actually intended to be covered with silk and varnish. I was spectacularly clumsy.

Owen was very keen on neat heads, tidy proportions. We used to spend much time at school tying flies after evening prep, bemusing if not amusing everyone. My finished products would be shown to him for inspection. 'No, the head's too big.' 'The proportions look wrong.' Then out would come the miserable razor, and I would try again, out of jealousy more than persistence. Owen taught me more than he knew.

At that time, the emphasis was on simple flies because it had to be: the Partridge family, endless Black and Peacocks, and hackled Greenwell's Glories. But they caught fish, these early efforts – enough trout to stimulate curiosity. The style of a hackled Greenwell, for example, could serve as a general pattern for other dry flies – Red Spinners, Pheasant Tails, Black Gnats. Hackles could be bunched to form wings; tails could be primped and set to give a particular list to the artificial; body materials could be doubled to form a thorax; feathers could be palmered; dubbing could be picked out. Before I knew it, I was knotting single strands of pheasant tail to tie Daddies, pairing slips of starling to form split wings, winding copper wire onto weighted nymphs, and copying shop-bought or *Trout and Salmon*-recommended patterns with the best and worst of them.

Then came entomology, Ireland, Newcastle and Coldingham. I can look into the flyboxes and trace my route, my fishing journey. I can see how far I have come, riddled with errors and muddle, looking for system in all the wrong places, recognising, ignoring and misconstruing – a fool with a magnifying glass and a tome on trout flies. Late in the day, I have realised that one has to reconstruct entomology from the trout's point of view, rather than going by the books. I spin on the lineaments of another

Hare's Ear, and smile gently. I look again into the flyboxes and watch the would-be purist tracing costal projections, head down. I remember how much I have forgotten, how much I have had to forget, and see the clutter of flies replacing that knowledge, reaching at last for the boy's simplicity and confidence. The death of an entomologist. Among the leaves of flies, I can remind myself that I was once lucky. And yet . . .

CHAPTER FOUR

Dark of
Midsummer

*A*nd yet there is still killing, game fishing's vast paradox on which all our occasions rest.

It is strange that I find this ethical problem most puzzling when I think of the sea trout. Of all fish, it lights my imagination and I sense its vulnerability. It is simultaneously a living poem and a responsibility. This sounds fanciful, but maybe it is not so strange: poems (at least, poems worth writing) must be responsibilities, and just as of all poetries I love the native and the Anglo-Saxon best, of all game fish I love the sea trout most. My mind moves along its seaward journey, past bladderwrack, sand and the curlew shores, then back along the spawning run with genetic intensity and turbulence, to the redds high in the far places where vivid green moss quakes unnervingly underfoot and the autumn sun glints on quartz ridges baffled by stray, thin clouds. There is enigma here, and loneliness, puzzle and need, the perennial and the provisional.

If I love the sea trout most, I know that Connemara

taught me to think of the fish in terms of weather, tide and beer-coloured floodwater. It taught me also of the sea trout's unpredictability, its moodiness, and its strength.

I have looked again over the old photographs: Owen's wild hair, my collection of crushed, famous hats; two brace of fish laid out on the stern thwart one lost, happy lunchtime; the days of good wave and broken light. These seem like another lifetime. Perhaps they were.

The sea trout are vanishing from the West. On virtually every fishery from Connemara to South Mayo (Cashla, Screeb, Inver, Gowla, Ballynahinch and Delphi) the same story mutters itself out in bars awash with dark theories: sandeels; greenhouse effects; poor spawnings; netting; afforestation; pollution; fish-farming and sea-lice; acts of God. The catch on each system has dwindled from hundreds, into tens, into single figures. On the winter redds, where once you could count fifty or sixty fish, there are now perhaps two, or one, or none. Much the same has been happening, drastic and unforeseen, on the Scottish west coast. The blue hotel boats lie rocking, raddled with grey stains of age and algae, like old faces rotting and unused. They fill with rainwater and hopelessness. The booking ledgers are ghosted by the faint pencil-lines of memory and midsummer hope. Now we live in drought and thin water. The rivers are empty, the long holidays somehow smaller. We have grown up and assumed our disappointments.

In the Irish west, the old gillies are gone and there is no-one to replace them. The young have migrated to Dublin and the market economies. There is no one sheltering under the rock at Lurgan, casually raising a hand to acknowledge another soft day, thank God. There are few with whom to discuss tomorrow's drifts; there are few that remember yesterday's. All that remains of the old ones are tangible epitaphs I think they would like: empty Guinness or Smithwick's bottles, gathering dust and spiders, stacked untidily in the damp corners of rainswept huts. Now even the huts are becoming part of the landscape, falling to decay.

The Mad Englishmen are gone too, the holidaying sur-geons who offered us lifts and who played bagpipes on the pier for no apparent reason, unless it was simply for the joy of being alive in Cashel as the evening light stained the bay with a discipline of red gold and the herons clumsily flapped across the mud of low tide to roost.

I remember the little Frenchman on the bridge at Gowla, who never forgot an introduction. '*Ici, Monsieur,*' I had said one drenched and fishless midnight, passing the hipflask. '*Je m'appelle Christophe. Cet homme est mon ami, Owen. Il est fou.*' The Frenchman grinned delightedly in the head-lights, his waistcoat dapper and whiskery with sedge. He has gone, too, into the dark of midsummer, but maybe he will remember the Irishman somewhere among the culture of his cognacs, and smile. His face, also, is hidden amid a crowd of stars.

Although there is no possibility of confidence, and no foundation for it, I feel the sea trout will survive. My opti-mistic angel prompts the theory that perhaps we are in the midst of some natural cycle which we are scarcely compe-tent to acknowledge. More pragmatically, we know the fish have survived elsewhere, in the rich waters of the east and along the coasts of the Irish Sea. They have survived, in particular, in river-systems whose estuaries are not tainted by salmon-farming and its accompanying pestilences. Yet here too the runs are becoming erratic. Smolts mysteriously migrate in millions, and then disappear. Fish entering the river may be wiped out *en masse* by poisonous seepages and acid drifts under the pine needles of young and thoughtless plantings. Even the fish in the estuaries, swirling in summer's midnights, are prey to nets, radio-activity, the vile burrowing of parasites and putrid human waste.

Still, somehow, the fish get through, late in our droughts, on the first of the autumn rains. The spawning redds, in places at least, will be tenanted anew. 'But,' comes back the whisper in the bar, 'for how long?'. Possibly, impossibly, it is already too late.

In luckier and more lucid summers, we fished for sea trout in the Scottish Borders and in Galloway; Esk, Annan, and Nith. It was a supplement to our early Irish education. We had been drawn to the Borders by *Trout and Salmon* reports ('250 fish averaging 2lb'), and in those days, the fishery reports had the ring of justification about them. The shamefaced puzzlement and depression that sometimes visit those same columns now were then only the future's guilty conscience.

The Border Esk is a quite beautiful river. It runs over rock ledges into green deeps, cool currents with the froth of the upstream quickness still upon them. Its banks are grey stone and shingle, or red sandstone cutting into the far banks like a cathedral buttress in a vast flood-working. In those deeps, and towards midnight in the draw of the pool tails, the fish lie (they used to lie) in squadrons, grey-blue fuselages of energy. And I wade out again into the darkened water.

Of all the excitement fly-fishing offers, nothing, nothing can compare with night-fishing for sea trout. Part of this excitement lies merely in the approach. By this I do not only mean the waiting time, that period between dusk and the first seven stars pricking out above the high cloud when fishermen sit on the bank and smoke, talk, or drink (or all three), before the serious business of the night begins. The approach starts weeks before, with the anxious scanning of the weather-maps, the tying of flies and the paring-down of tackle. There, look, is the low epicentre, just off Iceland, gathering isobars; it promises a flood. In the vice is the Medicine, or the Squirrel and Silver, or the marabou experiment you will keep in your box as a last bad resolution. Here, laid out, are the bits and pieces you keep in your pockets, or tuck into the pouch of your chestwaders: hookstone, spare nylon, a cheap torch that you hold in your mouth, a plastic gag of light and saliva . . . and the priest, uncomfortable implement.

You drive north, or take the train, subconsciously noting how the placenames begin to change structure as you near journey's end. These are names of Viking provenance, or names Celtic and inexplicable. The country of beck and ghyll, tarn, carn and carrick. The car pulls up gradients in low gears; the train takes the strain of the first moorlands, the quiet humps of the Howgills, beginning to purple. River courses steepen, and you try to catch a glimpse from a fast-moving window, your breath condensing on the glass like any traveller's imagination. You are going fishing. There will be nothing to do tomorrow except to think about fish, and you will lose yourself and all your bafflements in that one directed purpose.

The first time we arrived at the Esk, we had travelled over the Ribbleshead Viaduct to Carlisle, and from there by bus to Langholm, a trip of hayfever, delays, and upland barrens where, as the train hissed and sighed on its stop-overs, you could hear the grouse whirring away across the moor, alarmed – *hbrrrkoleklek* – and then the shunt of movement, the breath of the moor coming in through the carriage window, vaguely bitter. And fresh.

We decamped with rods and packs somewhere near Skipper's Bridge. As the bus pulled away, we were left in a forest silence on an empty road. Below, the Esk wound at low water over rocks scalloped by centuries, boulder-worn. Downstream, a sea trout leaped. I can still see its dark silhouette against the sky-reflecting water, and hear the pent *thwack* of its body pockmarking the stillness.

We walked along the road, down the pool, screened by trees, willow and alder, peering through the foliage. We could have foretold what we saw; we had already invented it in our memories. In the pool tail lay a shoal of sea trout, of between 2 and 4lb, with a goodly smattering of herling. A fish would occasionally turn from its place, and flash gold underwater in the midday light, or you would see that gold as energy, as a fish rushed to the surface to leap – a leaping sea trout's displacing shatter. Owen and I looked at each other, surprised, I suppose, by joy.

Part of sea trout fishing at night is ritual. The ritualistic aspects of fishing are, I think, some of the pastime's most important properties. They enable you to order and clarify tensions. Excitement is governed by propriety; imagination is, paradoxically, enlarged by discipline. Fishing becomes a kind of form.

It is much the same (or should be the same) with writing. Writing is, among other things, the exploration of a verbal game, and, as Auden once said, you cannot play a game without rules. These are not prescriptive rules – there are no prescriptions for creativity – but a set of benign structures whose presence you sense as an insistent rhythm or a telling image begins to demand attention. These structures are a gift from the past; you write in love and awareness, as you begin to find a freedom in form and structure. Language itself, not just literary language, is like this, too. Every day we construct infinitely many new sentences; what underlies this creativity is our tacit sense of the structure of English. We are rule-governed creatures, essential, habitual, creative, driven by things, words, moments we hardly understand.

And so we bring creativity to our fishing, and find, after all, that this creativity needs a sense of form, of ritual, in order to realise itself most deeply. With sea trout fishing, the rituals and proprieties are more keenly potent (and have more point) than in any other form of fishing known to me. I have already said something about the long-term approach, the weather-maps and the waiting vice. The short-term approach, the approach to and reconnaissance of the river, is equally a vital observance of form.

On the Esk, then as now, we walked the pools, stealthy in the sunlight. It is good if you can find a high bank, and move along it well-camouflaged, looking into the river – almost feeling your way underwater – with Polaroids. Sometimes a shoal of fish will give away their presence by leaping. At other times, most times, the fish will lie greyly underwater, breathing quietly, waiting to move that night, or run when the first hints of rain cool the night air. Or again, if you stand, or crouch, at a pool tail as night draws on, you may see the fish running, see the full gleam on their flanks as they turn across the fast water and into the draw, and perhaps see the merest hint of dorsal ripple as the fish slips into the pool and merges into the black water under the far bank.

Next there is the tackle, and another ritual. Everything has its pocket; you will need to find it quickly in the dark. There is food, and a flask for three in the morning when the fish have gone down and the early dawn is cold. There is whisky also, and tobacco, and a spare set of matches. And at the end of all other preparations there are the rod, reel and net. You check the net-sling; you pull all the line off the reel and rewind it snugly, with no fankled coils that might catch when a big fish decides to head for the sea; and you check the tip rings of the rod for grease, or caked-on fuller's earth, clearing them with a finger.

Finally, there is the walk down to the river across the dew-laden fields. You've had a solid supper-breakfast, and you feel heavy, hot and clumsy in waders. A heron, looking pale black and somehow mechanical in the twilight, flaps off at your coming. The woods are silent. In that silence, as you near the pool, you can hear the susurration of water, as if the river is breathing. You climb down onto the shingle. You put up the tackle as the bats freak the last light in the corner of an eye. Then you sit down, and wait.

The first evening on the Esk, we sat and waited, as ritual and common sense demand. The air darkened round us. Out in the Caul, a fish whirred a leap, frenetic. Then the branches parted behind us, and a disembodied set of wadered footsteps crunched on the shingle

He had appeared as if from nowhere, a small water spirit in a long mackintosh, his rod-tip dancing at the stars. 'Alright, boys.' He was Tommy.

Most rivers, I think, have their Tommys, their elderly sprites who have fished the pools since boyhood and have become, almost, part of the river, part of its folklore and part of its charm. Not all, however, are as patient or as knowledgeable. Tommy knew the Esk not just as he knew the back of his hand, but as well as he knew the rhythm of his own footsteps and the tenor and smell of all his comings and goings. The river was a constituent of him; it was necessary to him; he had it in him like memory or blood.

As we dogged him during our short, wet week, he taught us much; we learned as we watched him watch. He spent a great deal of time looking, thinking, seeing the sea trout although to our unaccustomed eyes they were invisible. When the river rose, and came down tea-coloured, he arrived with his big rod, a light link-leger and a green box of lobworms. As the river cleared, we would see him wandering down to Glen Firra with the fly-rod, the Langholm Silver clicked into the corks.

The worm was, without doubt, his favourite method. Yet there was none of the casual dunking one sometimes sees by the side of a sea trout stream in flood. He would wait, and choose his places with infinite care, often running the tackle down streams that looked unfishable, so fast and brown did they turn. But Tommy knew the trout were there, lying in a pause between stones, on the bottom in some scrape between rush and violence, and that is where he would fish, adjusting the weights on his leader so that the worm just bumped ground as it came towards him from where he had cast it gently upstream.

It was sheer finesse. He hooked the fish by watching the nylon, where it entered the water. I have tried since, many times, to emulate this, fishing the upstream worm for trout or, less frequently, for sea trout in the broken water of a big flood, and I have marvelled at the control and delicacy he brought to his fishing. It was an education in stealth and watercraft.

That was a short, wet week. The raindrops beat their

rudimentary and haphazard tattoo on the tent canvas. We were drenched by leakings and bootfuls in turn, and the river rose, and rose until it swamped the bankside grasses and brought down filth and branches from beyond Potholm, a watershed exacting its price. We lived on muesli, packet curries, and illicit Irish whiskey. Our greatest luxury was a boxful of fudge, which Owen's mother had lovingly tucked into his rucksack. This we ate sitting back-to-back on an airbed which was floating on rainwater that had collected on the tent's groundsheet. We talked fishing, and thought fishing, until finally we had caught a sea trout apiece, as the river fined down. For two dirty, wet, hungry and inevitable young fishermen, this was a giant success.

That next winter I left school, under clouds of my own making, and followed the sun to the hottest part of the world. In the Negev desert I watched scorpions and heard the dry ticking of desert spiders, some a handspan across, behind the bookshelves at night; something like the rustle of fear, or unhappiness. Yet into that hostile and burnished place I had taken one cherished possession: a box of sea trout flies, tied up for the Esk the year before. I suppose you know you have come of age as fisherman if you can take a box of trout flies into a desert pocked by minefields. Either that, or you are a fool; perhaps both.

The sea trout still run the Esk, as they run the Annan and the Nith; but they do not seem to run in either the numbers or the size that they did ten or even five years ago. Last year, as I escaped again from the dust of tension and disappointment, the hot hiss of work, I fished the Esk once more. The river ran slowly, and pale among the heat-stricken rocks; slime was gathering on the stream-bed. The drought had already gripped, and, although fish were in the river, they were reluctant to take. In one pool, a net-marked grilse swam crazily, on its side, damaged by contact and the deoxygenated water. In another pool in the upper river, sea trout were showing clear signs of distress. Only some pools in the lower river were reasonable to fish.

A run of some hundred sea trout had got through to Dead Neuk. Those who have fished this short pool will know of its depth, its stillness, and of the possibilities that it holds. In the slack draw of the tail, you can see the trout, lying in groups, just in from the sea beyond Longtown.

The river was alive and crowded with fishermen, most of whom walked down to Dead Neuk in the afternoon to watch the recently-run shoal of sea trout. That night, most of these same fishermen waded into the tail of Dead Neuk, right into the lies of the waiting fish. Next morning, the entire run of trout had been frightened out of their lies, and had moved uneasily upriver. I understand the pool did not fish well again for sea trout that season.

That example, of the crassest kind of fishing, is nowadays not confined to single instances; nor can it be put down to tyros' ignorance (the Dead Neuk anglers were hardly novices). I wonder if it is not merely greed, in which the absorption and responsibility of fly-fishing has been replaced by the imperatives of money, competition, and spurious prestige. Greed and folly replace 'I hope I'll catch a fish' with 'I must catch a fish', and devil take the hindmost. Yet even the hindmost barge into the darkened pool in wadersteps so clumsy they might be made with cloven hooves. A good persistence, that most necessary of fishing's desiderata, is replaced by a bad and meaningless pride.

I would not mind so much if it were not the sea trout which had suffered, and which will suffer again this year, and next, until all the pools are untenanted and all the anglers have driven away, complaining about the nets, the weather, the fish and each other. But these are no stocked rainbows, wonder of the finless-farm, and these are not waters which damage lightly. There are no replacements and very few remedies. The sea trout are a wild resource, and we still scarcely understand them. But, as in the

Scottish and Irish west, in the Border rivers too, they are vanishing before our knowledge can compass them. We cannot understand their future, or our own, unless we have first accepted and understood the critical lessons of the past and present.

Perhaps, after all, it is this which makes the mystery: the fact we know so little. What little we do know points towards some huge inter-connectedness, towards angling as an output of ecology.

Take the riddle of the sea trout's feeding. On some rivers, you fish for sea trout using long, streamlined flies which represent, it may be, the bait-fish of the sea trout's estuarial feeding-grounds, the sparling and sandeels. These tinsel-and-blue stylisations you fish wholly at night. On other rivers and other systems, you fish much smaller flies, perhaps a team of two or three size 10 or 12 bumbles or traditional patterns; but here again, you are fishing patterns which represent, it may be, the food of the sea trout's estuarial foraging – in this instance, crustaceans and sand-fleas. These small patterns you will fish during the day. In other words, sea trout of different systems will feed at sea in different ways, ways dependent on the availability of different kinds of food. When we fish for sea trout, we must be alive to those differences, and this in turn means that there can never be one single, all-encompassing approach (nor one ritual) which will be suitable for all sea trout fishing in all parts of these islands. Technique in time and place depends on the mystery of elsewhere, the turning of tides, the sea-feeding swirls under a midnight moon, how fish behave in their own times and places. It is precisely this particularity, this essential behaviour, which must run through the mind of the sea trout fisherman as he seeks to stimulate, to entice, to cajole those solid muscles of tide-beauty towards the moving artificial. Since we are dealing with the mystery of 'elsewhere', 'elsewhere' is where the mind must recreate itself: behind and beyond the short-term reconnaissance, behind and beyond the fly-tying vice and the weather forecasts, there is only the willed imagination, numinous and profound. A mind working like this, beyond prejudice and presupposition, and certainly beyond the barbs of success and failure, is committing to itself what is almost a spiritual act, a ground of being, at root wordless, pulled by a vast gravity just as the tides where the sea trout feed are dragged by the weight of a cold and unfledged planet. In that act of literal recreation, there is love.

I do not mean to say here that when I fish for sea trout I stare vacantly into the night, feeling transcendental and predetermined. I, too, am waiting for that sudden immediate weighing of the line in my hands. But if fly-fishing, and sea trout fishing as a zenith of that recreation, involves us in preoccupied abstraction and so becomes almost a way of life, then something numinous and profound has occurred; something has happened to alter 'the helthe of your body, and specyally of your soule'.

However, where there is love, there is also disappointment and loss. Love and imagination measure themselves, and define themselves, against their absence. So I return again to diminution, to the droughts and vanishings where the sea trout are gone, to guilt, and killing, and responsibility. I look into the future and see miles upon miles of orange-buoyed drift-net, wickedly knotted into a small mesh; I see fish floating, belly-up; the spectrum-hues of petrol and oil-slick; the brown river so acid it is fish-lethal; the empty estuaries where limp tissue tangles in poisonous kelp and where sea-lice burrow into smolt flesh; the dying colonies of starving sea-birds; the sick, viral flood; a last, solitary sea trout, spawn-locked, on a silt-choked redd.

Perhaps in another ten years I will look back at this and shake an older head at my synchronic sense of crisis; I wish that shall be so, and wish it with intensity. Yet so much of sea trout fishing seems now to be yesterday's, the rod up and shuddering to bend in the stars of earlier decades. While it is true that research into the sea trout's decline has recently if belatedly got underway, perhaps we probe only what is terminal, and are already bereaved. We have already lost so much; and while great love prospers with understanding, it also needs hope, and time to grow. But we seem to have little hope, and no time, and growth is cir-cumscribed by the pressures of 'success', measured in column-inches in the angling reports.

In the meantime, caught in our rituals and vices, we shall walk down to the river at August low, and wait on, into the dark of midsummer, surrounded by the quiet voices of our previous selves, and hear, far down the pool in the last light, the tired slosh of a sea trout coming to a waiting net, and see the torch prick on over the far shingle, and a crouching half-silhouette of a fisherman, who slips the fish into his bass, stands, and slowly wades out again into the darkened water.

CHAPTER FIVE

Arguments and Reasons

Yet there is still killing, still tarnished pride. Beyond all the despairs and bad symptoms, the shrunken summers and the nadirs of the fishery reports, there are still our own, local actions, motivated by principles that range from the almost inexpressible to the frankly callous. At the heart of those principles, there is the issue of killing, and fly-fishing's status as a pastime.

Fishing is almost by definition a bloodsport, and this word is defined in turn as meaning 'any sport involving the killing of an animal, esp. hunting'. Whatever gauze of semantic quibbling can be weaved around that, it is impossible to deny that fly-fishermen kill. For some of us today, however, killing fish – the raised priest, death's quivering metals in our wet hands – has become a series of increasingly uncomfortable instants, dark in the memory.

Our ancestors would not have been so puzzled or chastened. The author of the 15th-century *Treatise*, or Walton, or the ebullient Cotton, or the great Hawker who raked wet flies across the Test from the back of a horse, would scarcely have understood the term 'bloodsport', or the need for it. It is not the case, I think, that they fished in times that were more bloodthirstily uninhibited than ours; we can hardly claim that from our perspective late in this troubled century. Their indifference and apparent carelessness stems, surely, from the fact that they fished and lived among a greater abundance, in the days when salmon still ran the Thames and Trent and catches of trout had to be numbered in the evening on the fingers of several hands. It stems, too, from the fact that they were living and writing, if not in Europe's springtime, then in its long Indian summer, when leaves were still green and when perhaps it must have seemed that there were whole seasons of curious discovery ahead. Even in living memory, our Edwardian grandsires, tweed-clad among their holiday estates, hardly felt a squeamishness about huntin', shootin', and fishin' – relics of an old pronunciation which reflect a more spacious and perhaps a less self-conscious age.

Now it is autumn and the time of falling fruit. Rivers are dirty, rain is bitter and acid, the salmon run erratically and the wild trout are gone from the lowlands. Our acres of inherited future have constricted to a patch of suburb scrub, and air has shrunk with them like hope. Tomorrow is an autoclave of pressure – pressure on time, on work, on the town and on the country – and it will leave behind, unless we dare otherwise, a vacuum of bad dreams and might-have-beens. The nightmarish, the apocalyptic, are closing round our heads. As yet, we sense them, waiting in the rainforests, as a malevolent absence in the ozone layer. They have not yet become actual presences, have not put on their disastrous rags and infested bandages, but they are walking towards us with their arms open. A sick, sweet smell invades our hot and airless afternoons.

Small wonder then that in this dwindling time, killing has begun to vex so many of us, the fishermen. Surrounded by casual destruction, implicated in the intrigues of money and day-ticket greed, aware that fly-fishing is becoming tainted by competition, we ourselves become corrupt. I am no exception.

Many close seasons ago, in 1988, I started idly to look over my fishing diaries, kept since 1969. This is of course a proper retrospective thing to do during the winter, but stupidly I kept a tally; so many trout taken during this year, fewer taken the next ('a drought year'), more taken the next, and so on. In all, I reckoned I had fished seriously for trout with fly for fifteen seasons (since 1973). My count of takeable fish reached, I realised with a small frisson of almost-delight, one thousand and a half (half a white trout which Owen and I had jointly outmanoeuvred on the trail on one of Screeb's bad days). It was a milestone of sorts, and worth a Scotch or two. I sat back in the chair with malt on my tongue, and began to congratulate myself. Naturally, I knew that there are many fly-fishers who catch this number of trout in a couple of seasons, let alone fifteen years, but still, I felt a certain spurious pride in the roundness of the number and in the accuracy of the diaries.

Then I thought about what I had just done. I had reduced a complex joy to some Biro-jottings and statistics on the back of an envelope. Whole tracts of fascination had been evaluated by the dead-weight of fish flesh. For years I had been (and am yet) vaguely sickened by rows of stricken trout laid out below the kind of self-congratulatory smile that you find (or used to find) in some of the fishing monthlies. That smile was now mine. Not for the first time where fishing is concerned, I suddenly felt clumsy and ignorant. I closed the diaries and put them away. The after-taste of the malt was metallic, like blood.

This discomfiting episode took place a short time after the trip to Driffield invoked earlier – the day of the dying grayling – and it fed my malaise and disappointment. I began to think hard about the ethics of fly-fishing.

'Ethics' is a grand word, about which resonate other grand words and grandiloquent phrases: purpose, principles, responsibility, moral choices, codes of conduct, right

65

and wrong. Is it too serious-minded to consider these high and stern matters in connection with something as simple and (in one sense at least) something as primitive as fishing? I think not – not now, in this dwindling time, when fishing is under palpable threat. 'Take A Friend Fishing' urged the poster that I saw last summer tacked up on a clubhouse wall. Yes, take a friend, live out that buzz-word, solidarity. If you don't, the subtext runs, there's no security in solitary enjoyment. And then; fishing will be laid to rest, and a short farewell.

Ethics. The word reverberates like the sounded pipe of a cathedral organ, echoic, enormous and surprising. But it is a word which fly-fishermen should consider, for both public and private reasons. I do not mean to say that fishermen should mope towards the water's edge feeling laden and portentous, but that we should attempt to understand ourselves, and the relation between us and our chosen means of solace.

I will begin in a curious place, and with a curious fish, the gudgeon. Between my early incarnation as a minnow-expert, and my later metamorphosis on Harden Beck, I fished seriously for gudgeon in the Leeds-Liverpool canal. There was something about that canal. It was partly the smell, of damp, mossed brickwork, motor oil and mud; it was partly its look of dank disuse. The canal was hardly lucid like a chalkstream or tranquil like a lake, but was neglected, productive, and ugly; odd plastic bags swayed gently in it, wind-driven bits of polystyrene skimmed inexplicably past on it, half-bikes mysteriously appeared in it, and prams, and even, on one unforgettable morning, a Morris 1000 with red leather upholstery, greenly submerged in a good roach swim.

The canal was resolutely industrial, its surface tainted with rainbow slicks, or frothed with suds where the water fell several feet into a lock bottom. At the usual place by the lock outfall I eventually learned to catch gudgeon, on a single maggot or small red worm snicked onto a size 18 crystal-bend hook. At the end of the afternoon when the net was raised there would be fifty or sixty gudgeon wriggling there. Rarely would there be other fish: a few small, bright roach in their vivid mail-scales and Dulux-sunset fins, or the bristling hand-spans of a perch or two. But these red-letter catches were, typically, scarce, and it was invariably the obliging gudgeon which made up the netful. They were about as long as my middle finger, snub-headed and greedy, although one monster was nearly six inches long; he was played as carefully as I would now play a big sea trout. All were taken on the same stick float, 2lb line, and with a couple of number 6 shot near the hook. The important thing was to fish light, and to keep the bait on the bottom. In this respect, gudgeon fishing has not changed in three hundred years. That connoisseur of quietism, Isaak Walton, wrote that the gudgeon 'is an excellent fish to enter a young Angler, being easie to be taken with a small red worm, on or very near to the ground'. One young angler was certainly entered on the gudgeon, on that morose canal where the grey sky bloomed in the green water and there was charm in dereliction.

This seems an unpromising place to begin an analysis of ethics, but it is relevant insofar as catching those gudgeon needed a rudimentary kind of understanding. This fish bit better in the oxygenated water below the lock than in the slow, backed-up water above it; they bit better 'very near to the ground'; they had their times, and their seasons. After a while, I knew every detail of the swim; the clump of old iron which snagged the line, the edge of the three-foot drop-off. That short stretch of canal was to me then what, say, a known drift on Shiel or a cast on the Wharfe is to me now – full of promise, the imagination reconstructing itself underwater. And this is the point; if we are to succeed in catching gudgeon, or sea trout, or indeed any other wild fish, we must first have *understood*. This understanding implies a long process, vast tracts of time filled with reading and thinking – before the rod bends. It also implies empathy: wind-knowledge; tide-knowledge; birds and insects . . . and fish. These implications mean that the given definition of the term bloodsport ('. . . killing of an animal, esp. hunting') is too restrictive. It excludes all the effort, understanding and skill which bring the invisible quarry briefly close.

There is a corollary here. Many of us spend hours each winter tying flies. When I tie an Invicta or a Soldier Palmer, I am not thinking of a trout lying dead on the boards. I am thinking of the sedge – caddis, pupa, and adult – and still summer evenings after rain, night moving in across the fields, and the trout beginning to show excitedly after a dour afternoon. In thinking like this, I become my own future's shadow; I recreate myself elsewhere. Aesthetic folly this may be, but one thing is certain: in tying up James Ogden's magnificent pattern, I have not committed a bloodsport. Therefore, and by an inescapable logic, fishing, and all that goes with it, need not immediately imply killing. That equation would do us a disservice. As the great angler and observer, Sidney Spencer, wrote: 'the rewards of our vocation as anglers cannot be measured in terms of dead fish'.

Even so, this does not exhaust the term 'bloodsport', far from it, and the second term in this troublesome compound is worth examination. Is fly-fishing indeed a sport? My instincts tell me now, although they have not always done so, that it is not. It is what the *Treatise* called it, not a sport but a disport, a pastime.

I once fished with a man for whom fly-fishing was a sport, a matter of competition, one-upmanship, cups, teams and champions. Cups, teams and champions were his sole topics of conversation, and it was a little disconcerting to share a boat all day with the man and find that, after all, he was a fishing bore. He had competed on each of the big waters – Chew, Rutland, Leven – but for him, a good drift did not mean a drift which sets the mind alight, the ground shallowing from the deeps into a reed-fringed bay with a sandbar across its mouth; it meant a drift over which he had taken so many rainbows and browns the week or the month before, so winning the match (or playing the starring role in his team's performance). Everything about him seemed glossy and self-confident. His rods, three of them, gleamed lustrously; his varnished wooden flyboxes were full of fluorescence. Every time he cast, it was a performance. On the water we fished together, he took just one wild brown late in the afternoon, and despised it as not worth his attention.

I compare him with another fisher I met recently at Blagdon. He arrived at the lake in a battered old Austin A30, with makeshift rod-holders Scotch-taped to the roof. We saw little of him thereafter, apart from watching him land one good fish from afar. We were too preoccupied with the sun and the flat calm, and Blagdon's lifeless Top End. But in the evening, we met again in the carpark, which was quiet and dismal; everyone had blanked. 'Do any good?' I asked. 'Well,' he said, Welsh and knowing, 'it wass my last trip of the season, and do you know' (bringing out the fish) 'I had a few.' He had four, all taken on a little dry sedge of his own tying. 'Moving in clumps they wass,' he said. 'All I had to do was get the cast right, see?' He slid the fish onto the bottom of the car, and took down his rod, which was cane with a slight set in it. 'Yes, last trip of the season, nice to see a fish or two . . .' His voice tailed off, and he paused, turning back to look at the lake. Then, almost to himself, he murmured 'Not bad for nearly eighty'. He recollected himself, stooped, and drove off into the evening in his muttering car. There had been a strange brightness in his eyes as he had said goodbye.

For the competitors, fly-fishing may be a sport. For the eighty-year-old Welshman it was a pastime, skilled and savourable. I do not mean that those fishermen who prefer competition are less than skilled – some are gifted beyond my dreams – but that I doubt, even mistrust, their sense of priorities. In my own thinking, for what it is worth, it is the

69

fish that come first every time, not trophies and envies and the cold machinery of win or lose. Caught in that machinery, the fish – whether rose-moled and stippled, or tailless and stupid – become mere counters, abstract entities better dead. No, I do not like the idea of fly-fishing matches. Whatever rules they are fished under, whatever selectivity this involves, in competitions, fishing and killing are made too nearly synonymous, and that synonymity is hard to reconcile with the charm of a reflective ethic.

Bloodsport. I wonder if there are not a couple of further points that can be disentangled from the web? First, I am puzzled by the relationship between fly-fishing and the other bloodsports, hunting and shooting. I think of these three rather as I think of the kinship between three languages – say, English, German, and Dutch. All three spring from the same root, and share generic similarities. They may even share items of vocabulary. Yet the three bloodsports, like the three languages, are formally distinct. Each has its own native speakers, as it were, its own loyalists (and rebels), and the commerce between the three is of a relatively limited kind. But if fly-fishing is formally distinct, in what does its distinctiveness lie?

Part of the answer must focus, surely, on the fact that in approaching the trout with a fly, we are attempting to persuade it into a response, a positive choice. (Perhaps 'positive response' is a more accurate term, since the word 'choice' has connotations of reasoning, and it may be inaccurate to talk of reasoning where fish are concerned.) With shooting, or hunting, positive response is not at a premium. A bird, for example, is either shot, winged (a nasty, distressing image), or missed; a fox is either run to earth, or it outmanoeuvres the dogs and escapes. These respective quarries, however, have hardly been persuaded through guile – unless under the broad heading of 'guile' we admit camouflage and decoys and the esoteric, if compelling, accoutrements of wildfowling. With fly-fishing, however, we seek out the undisturbed living, in its natural environment, and act in order to deceive, to persuade a trout into a positive response. The definition of fly-fishing offered earlier (page 26) marries well with this point, and also implies dexterous subtlety, a conjuring with fur and feather allied with understanding and no small mechanical skill – and yet, as we all know, trout are often undeceived.

Taken together, then, these issues suggest that fly-fishing is formally unlike its relatives in the family of bloodsports. Connected, too, with this theoretical distinctiveness is a practical hiatus. Fly-fishermen ultimately rely for the particulars of their sport on themselves, and but rarely on other agents. We have no horses (unless we are Hawkers) and no dogs or beaters to take us to the invisible quarry or bring it near. Certainly, there are keepers, gillies, pundits, and other water-managers, but ultimately, at least, fly-fishermen are solitary hunters, adepts of intensive concentration, and our collateral spirits, the keepers and gillies, may be kindred but they are still collateral. We must, after all, come back to the cardinal point that it is only fishermen who offer their quarry something to which that quarry may, or may not, respond. Thus, it seems that bloodsports do share a kinship; but members of any family are marked by difference, and the relationship between hunting, shooting and fishing is no exception.

Again, bloodsports, of whatever kind, rest on an enormous paradox, and this paradox is seen at its purest in fishing. We might agree, for instance, that fishing involves empathy, imagination and care. It also, sometimes, involves pain, blood, and destruction – destruction of just those creatures it is our passion to understand. We do, undeniably, kill, and if we do, we eat; we are fascinated by the process. But the price of that fascination, and also its embodiment, is what lies stiffly in the freezer or lusciously on the plate. That is the paradox: we kill what we have most sought to enjoy and to understand. We might even ask if that little aphorism could be reversed: do we enjoy what we kill? What motivates the paradox?

Here I shall be heretical, and suppose that Isaak Walton was wrong when he wrote 'As no man is born a poet, so no man is born an angler'. There are two ways of looking at this rather gnomic statement, and both of them suggest that in this instance, Walton's quiet enthusiasm had betrayed him. First, Walton is clearly speaking metaphorically. No man indeed can be born a poet or an angler (although I wonder about some of my fishing friends, several of whom must have arrived at the natal hospital with a full set of tackle and a fistful of day-tickets). What is at stake, then, is the metaphorical truth of Walton's statement. The assessment of that truth depends on asking the question whether angling (and writing) are matters of latent capacity, or matters of opportunity and practice. Walton, I think, implies the latter. In this he is a man of his time, a new rationalist (and contemporary of Descartes) with a firm belief in training, instruction and learning. In short, he implies that angling, and poetry, can be taught. Perhaps in his view, they are relatively mechanical arts. Walton's *Lives of the Poets* tends to support this argument. His emphasis throughout is not on 'genius' nor transcendental skill ('genius' was a word appropriated only by a later age) but on family, upbringing, education, training and hard work.

The poet Donald Davie, speaking of the craft of writing, once commented that 'poetry can be taught – but not to everyone'. There are those for whom the line-break, that cardinal principle of verse-writing, is and remains an aural mystery, just as there are those pianists for whom musical phrasing (and pedalling) seems to remain obscure. Similarly, not everybody can be taught to fish, particularly not to fly-fish. Using the fly tellingly is not merely a matter of training and practice (although of course these refine our rudimentary skills). There is nothing too surprising about this. There are those who are born with an abstract talent for chess, or mathematics, music or writing; others are born with what seems to be an instinctive understanding of weather, or machinery, or the opposite sex. As C.G. Jung and others have pointed out, we are driven not just by the immediate genetic past but by ancestral histories, ancestral voices and preconceptions: our latent tendencies are the results of conspiracy down the grey, running centuries.

We could do worse than to look here for what is often called 'the hunting instinct'. Perhaps this instinct lies deep, far back not in our own pasts but the history of the race, never coming to full consciousness. Perhaps, just perhaps, it might be an innate potential – but crucially, this potential will be realised differently in different people. Just as there will be those for whom long division, or the appropriate moment to castle, or musical phrasing, will remain mysterious, so there will be people in whom the hunting instinct is dormant, or entirely absent.

But talk of 'the hunting instinct', or the image of the fisherman as solitary hunter, can be overdone. Typically, for instance, the best fishermen I know are those who in their professional lives are adept at making abstract connections, at conceptualising in the broadest terms. (In this sense it cannot be accidental that writers, poets, academics and philosophers figure so strongly in fishing's literature.) The 'hunting instinct' can certainly be fostered by training and education, but at root it is primarily a matter of vision. I do not think everyone has the speculative gift of such vision; I wish I possessed more of it myself. And I come back once more to the paradox of killing and enjoyment. If vision, if connection and connectedness, are at the root of our instincts, then this cannot be a partial vision. It must include dawns and dusks, low and high water, droughts and floods, spawning and predation, time and tide, wind and weather, fly-life, fur and feather, tackle, technique, and trouble. It is precisely this understanding which, as I claimed earlier, brings the quarry close. Yet the deeper the understanding, the more responsibility accompanies it. Caught in that understanding, we are also caught up in the movement of the seasons, the migrations of fish, the endlessly joined solitudes that go to make up the

system of which we are a part. It is surely this of which the
fly on the water, or the float unperturbed on its slow ripple,
is symbolic. As the fly disappears in a quick thirl of water,
as the float jags away among the lily-pads, there! The lift of
the rod connects you with a different living; there is the
shock of contact; the guessed-at world, coveted and numinous, has become live and visible. There is, too, as the rod
pulses again under the corks, the satisfaction that theory
has translated into specifics. The equation has been solved;
the king is check-mated; the phrase is perfect.

There are deeper, but more practical and less symbolic
connections. As we fish, and as we come to understand our
fishing, we know that we are implicated in what we enjoy.
The link between fish and fisherman is more than a taut
line. Fishermen, more than governments (and certainly
more capably), know which disasters threaten the environ-
ments in which they find their deepest enjoyment. If you
are a salmon or sea trout fisherman you know the dangers
posed – and now all too real – by pollution, by estuarial
fish-farming, by netting on the high seas. If you fish for
trout you know of the problems entailed by chemical fertil-
isers; by abstraction; by unchecked predation of mink or
goosander. Fishermen are the closest links society has with
some of the most important constituent parts of the
environment we have inherited and whose care is
entrusted to us. It is little good pretending that the public at
large, or one political party, can care effectively for this
environment and its smaller localities – its catchments, river
valleys, estuaries, spawning beds and feeder streams.
Anglers know the importance of these places and the hope
they bring. They know too that any loss in any part of the
environment and its food chain has incalculable effects on
the whole. So, even if we are, or like to think of ourselves
as, solitary hunters, we are also responsible for the
conservation entailed by the enjoyment of killing. Such
conservation does not mean stocking a lorry-load of fish
once-yearly. It implies study of habitat; study of past litera-

ture; remedial action; commitment. Hunting is also strategy; if fishing is a bloodsport, it also wears a managerial face whose future lies in the conservation of the aquatic environment. It is in this final image – the angler as conservationist, as thinker and strategist – that tomorrow must rest, as we attempt to clarify our pastime. The end must be seen to justify the means.

For myself, I know that these means include killing, but they also include care and voluntary restraint. These days, for example, I find it difficult to fish for anything that cannot be eaten. I spend more time fishing selectively, since I cannot pardon myself for causing distress to creatures I will subsequently release. I spend more time on study of the life in lakes and rivers, rather than on technology. These, I should say at once, are purely personal choices, attempts to find some reasonable way through the painful semantics of 'any sport involving the killing of an animal, esp. hunting'. Whether I was, or was not, born an angler, I know that learning to make such choices has taught me more about myself, and more about fishing, than blood and the priest.

As I write this it is mid-January. The grayling season is drawing to a close, and, even if I could afford them, the spring runs of salmon are far away. Floods hurl down the river valleys, and Scotland is drawn blinds and blizzards. Yet I know, with a certain and almost happy confidence, that high on the redds, life will have begun again. What has just been born among storms and snow-drifts will, perhaps, run invisibly past me in the coming years, or leap in a scatter of displaced silver, or rise in the corner of an impossible place that my misguided cast will never reach. There is always, beyond ethics, this difficult, fragile continuity. Tomorrow – motivated, paradoxical, dialectic and bizarre – I will take down the rods, open last season's flyboxes, and scan the diaries, ignoring the statistics. I will begin to dream.

CHAPTER SIX

Days of the
Black Dog

*T*hey all come to puzzle us, the days of the black dog. They begin as moments, minutes, hours – as fankles and chastenings, of freaks and accidents, of snappings, stings and miseries. They continue as blanks, as baleful losses, spookings, scarings, carelessness. They end in the bottle and the curt note, the dismal diary, the dark in the mind.

I do not know who invented the phrase 'the black dog'. Something prompts me to the idea that the words are a low Churchillian growl at disappointment, but the metaphor is apt whatever its origins. The black dog, its eyes staring at mist; the black dog, whining behind your shoulder; the black dog, a pointless presence, but ailing and avid. The black dog; the bad, bad dog-days.

You will not catch fish while the black dog walks in your head. You may have read everything in sight. You may wade silently; cast like an angel. Your split-winged dry-fly may kiss the water, perfectly cocked. You may hook fish with a split-second turn of the wrist. You may even play them, with the rod nodding appreciatively high at the sky or the shrouded stars. But you will scarcely, if ever, land a trout, and your creel will always be light. If this is true for trout, it is even more true of fishing for sea trout. (My infrequent experiences with salmon tell me also that when the black dog yelps, the seasons pass salmonless.)

I am expert in nothing but the black dog. I will put this foul creature together for you, limb by limb, eye by eye.

The first leg of the beast is simple ignorance. Wise, as always, after the event, by the time you write up your fishing notes you will have discovered that the fish you plied for hours were not taking the hatching midge but hatching sedges along with floating snails on their hot, silent migrations. Or perhaps you flailed away the best part of the day over a reach of the river which only hours before had been host to a carnival of bathing children and stick-chasing, unblack and all-too-real dogs. Or perhaps you have visited a much-advertised lake ('stocked with rainbows, best fish 6lb 7oz') without realising that the famous stocking takes place once a year, in March. Your visit was in September. Or perhaps you have put up part of your holiday money on a boat-ticket for a lake, loch, or lough in the high, good country, and driven for hours over axle-smashing tracks, and then walked, heavy and sweating, into the wilderness, only to find that the boat key is still on its nail in the estate office . . . and that there is no boat and that the shoreline is a boot-sucking bog. Or your beat on the river was polluted last Thursday with slurry, or Cymag. Or your lake, loch or lough has suffered so badly from acidification that it is barren. Or that the Water Authority sent down a vast artificial flood on the afternoon of your let. And you have discovered that people still take good money from you for these disasters.

But these are circumstantial kinds of ignorance. The most important kind is surely an ignorance about hatches, or tides and weather – I suppose in that increasing order of importance, depending on the fish you set out to catch, but then again, maybe in no particular order at all.

'Matching the hatch' is, I think now, an over-rated pursuit. But sometimes – already the black dog is licking its one paw – accuracy can be essential. This seems particularly true on rivers. When the iron blue are up, it is seldom any use plying the trout with a daddy long-legs (I have tried); when sedges scuttle into the darkness, it is nugatory to fish a size 22 midge pattern (I have tried). Or again, on the lakes . . . but on the lakes you have perhaps more margin for error: fish taking hatching midges will sometimes take a decent pattern of traditional wet fly, so long as there is sufficient wind to disguise the deception. Fish taking fry – those leviathans of the season's end, swirling in at the piers round your feet – will sometimes gently swallow a sparsely-dressed Pheasant Tail nymph, although why this is I have no idea. On the stocked waters, of course, there is always the possibility of what we black dog experts call a daft 'un. Yet even the daft trout, half-crazed and fin-cracked, sometimes need accurate presentation, if not accurate patterns. The black dog will begin to grin at you, and your casting will go to pieces. Your carefully greased leader will sink; your fast-sinking line will float. Your toes will start to curl.

Then there are tides and weather. I rarely give advice, and certainly not about fishing, but I can tell you this: never fish a river that flows backwards.

I will say something about such a river. It began as a miracle, and ended as a marsh. This river contained sea trout. It is a famous sea trout river, somewhere northerly and westerly. I know it contained sea trout because – after a long, fishingless summer – I saw them: slow shapes, slow, dimly-moving shapes under the bridge in the shadows of a late afternoon. These fish were huge. I could feel a pulse going in my temple. With two friends, I walked on air to the relevant hotel and bought a ticket.

We prospected, tackled up, waited, began to fish. The breeze had followed us into the twilight and became a gale. I shall have more to say about wind shortly, but this was a blind, dark, salt-bearing wind to rip up marram grass and put white horses into the trees. Branches began to crack. At the same moment, the fly-line dragged in my hands, moving upstream. The gale crackled. What was sand under my studs became a thick, viscous mud. A tidal bore tipped quickly over wader-tops. The gale and the water clabbered as I began to sink. It seemed a long danger to the bank – to the shore. It was almost a fatal danger – among the constant thrashing of the trees, as squall after squall turned in the night air and became lunatic; as the river flowed backwards on the night tide.

Certainly, it was ignorance. I realise now, the hairs rising on the nape of my neck, that it could have killed. But happily, there are more benign kinds of tide-ignorance, and they are also more frequent: on your rare, expensive visits elsewhere, for example, local knowledge will inform you that the sea trout will not run (a) on spring tides, (b) on neap tides, (c) when the tide is ebbing, (d) when the tide is flooding, and in any case (a Grand Slam of black dogs) the fish you saw when the tide was ebbing or flooding, neap or spring, were, after all, mullet. I have fished for hours over mullet with big sea trout flies, hungover at three o'clock on a bleak July morning. I do not recommend this as a pastime.

Then there is weather. By weather I mean wind.

> There are certain precautions – though none of them very
> reliable –
> Against the blast from bombs, or the flying splinter,
> But not against the blast from Heaven, *vento dei venti*,
> The wind within a wind, unable to speak for wind . . .
>
> (Henry Reed, from 'Chard Whitlow')

Wind persecutes me whenever and wherever I fish. My diaries and memory are littered with it, like-words become leaf-fall: 'drifting impossible because of fluky wind'; 'fishing difficult because of malevolent squalls'; 'white horses everywhere'; 'took two of us to row – then abandoned boat'; 'high wind – lost drogue'; 'blown off bicycle on way'; 'lost hat'. And so on.

I do not mean simply 'A Windy Day'. 'A Windy Day' is a pleasure in the country. What I mean are the blasts from Heaven and Hell, the winds that come from the forsaken nether parts of the earth, winds that blunt your eyeballs and that dunt dumbly in your eardrums.

It begins innocently enough. The morning's ignorance is, if not quite bliss, then at least quietly pleasant. The day promises great things: you look out of the window and see the barest stirrings of twigs and telephone wires. A good fishing day, you think, promising a wind neither too little nor too much. Then you drive or walk towards the water, and notice the roadside trees beginning to nod rather glee-fully at wind-ripples forming on puddles. Then the willows turn pale side out and begin to heave on their stumps. The car is buffeted by gusts. Elsewhere, pylons are down. It is unadvisable to put out in a boat. You creep – you are forced to creep – miserably around in the bankside vegeta-tion, getting stung, catching the fly in blown stalks. The lake rears in its dark and storm-driven waters. The insect life underwater is semi-concussed. The trout are absent. The black dog drags itself towards you on its first limb, the bitter wind foul on its breath.

The second leg of the animal is incompetence. Ignorance and incompetence – two eyes peer viciously at you now in your fishing nightmares, assume a face. One of the masks of Cerberus.

Possibly the largest trout I have ever hooked drew the line gently on a Leaded Shrimp in a difficult place. As the rod went up, there was that sudden, heavy silence – none of the spectacular, meaningless thrashing that takes place sometimes with fish of a pound or two. The fish, boring deep, ran straight upstream, into a sunken, long-aban-doned tractor wheel. It took a timed ten minutes of sweat and light pressure to coax the fish out. Then there we were, in open water, with the fish running. As the coils of loose line drew taut through what Skues called 'the arch of beauty', I stood on the rest of fly-line. No ballet dancer could have reacted more swiftly. But as the line tightened into my crotch, I knew my one-legged performance was being watched by two black, dogged eyes. I was right.

I think the black dog lives and sickens in certain places. In exactly the same spot – snags, tractor wheel, weed – I hooked another big trout almost exactly one year later. I beat this fish and was even drawing it towards me. There was a sudden manic flapping of large, whistling wings, and a persistent, vicious hiss. The swan certainly meant business. I am incompetent with swans; I will go a long way to avoid a cygnet. So, incompetently, I abandoned the rod, the fish, the play, and fell back into the nettles. This performance was followed by an immediate thunderstorm. I was not waterproof.

If these kinds of incidents are repeated, they have a creeping insidious effect on all your fishing. You are prey to minor incompetences, like taking the wrong flybox – ending up on a beck with just one salmon fly you must salvage from the mud and the moths of your hat-brim. You will drive three hours to a chalkstream and find, as you undo the tyings of the rod-bag, that you have brought the wrong implement: it is a broken beachcaster. You will open your expensive aluminium fly-case and fumble, and then watch as your precious collection of paraduns sinks laughingly into a deep eddy. On the first day of your expensive stillwater holiday you will knock the landing-net over the downwind gunwale. You will hook the back of your sweater – the sweater with the oiled, close-knit weave which an aunt bought you last birthday, and which, once it catches a barb, will never let go. Under the gaze of the black dog, it becomes a Venus fly-trap of low fashion. Or you will hook the back of someone else's sweater just as they are fishing intently for the trout, the only trout, that has that moment risen at the side of the boat. Or, drifting expansively on some loch patronised by the well-heeled with binoculars, you will put down the rod and allow your team of three to drag behind the boat while you reach for the baler to relieve an uncomfortable bladder. Something mighty with whirring fins will seize your dragging point-fly, and the rod will dance on the boards and then disappear with a slack, hollow splosh. Ten pairs of accountants' eyes will watch you trap the landing-net in your zip.

You may think I am romancing, gilding, decorating the truth. Two glinting dog-eyes watch me as I say this: these things happen, and will go on happening. Others have known them, even the august and the numinous unknown dead. Ignorance – of hatches or conditions – and incompetence. Mark them all well.

One of my favourite passages of fishing writing comes in the pages of the 15th-century *Treatise of Fishing with an Angle*. In this great work, the author gives a list of what he (or perhaps she) tactfully calls 'Impediments':

The twelve impediments which cause men to catch no fish, apart from other common causes which may happen by chance, are these. The first, if your tackle is not good and well-made. The second is if you do not angle in biting time. The third, if the fish are frightened by the sight of any man. The fourth, if the water is very thick, white, or red as lees [dregs], from any flood recently fallen. The fifth, if the fish will not stir either for cold or fair weather. The sixth, is if the water is very hot. The seventh, if it rains. The eighth, if it hails or snows. The ninth, if there is any tempest of any storm. The tenth, if there is a great wind from any direction. The twelfth, if the wind is from the north or northeast or southeast; for generally, both in winter and in summer, if the wind blows from any part of these points, the fish will not usually bite nor stir.

From the translation in John Macdonald's Quill Gordon
(Knopf: New York, 1972)

It is a magnificent, all-inclusive summary (although the eleventh impediment has been lost), and I particularly admire the nice distinction between a 'tempest' and 'a great wind' . . . from any direction. I include this passage because I have lived it in its entirety. Perhaps we might say that the third leg of the black dog is made from these overall set of conditions, a set that includes wind and floodwater, but which also embraces sullenness and silence, clumsiness and bad temper, biting time and the time of no biting. Conditions: a c-word. The two eyes of the beast now see, gaze blindly into the future, looking for you, recognising you from the past.

Many years ago now, before the stock collapse, when sea trout still ran in numbers into the uplands of the far north-west, a group of us set out for a week's fishing on Loch Shiel. It is a magnificent water, stricken and made by mountains and cloud, and is reached by a drive that takes you through Glencoe and across the Corran ferry, Scotland's tartan and twilight. After a summer storm, the glens are lit by successions of rainbows, green prisms and arcs among the high dissolving mist, and your spirits rise along with the rising flood, running with the salmon and sea trout from the Atlantic into the brawling, tended river, past its fishing piers and deeps and into the loch at Acharacle and beyond, slowly tenanting each of the lies: Rabbit Bay, Coul Bay, Grilse Point, and Polloch, with its sheer walls, its entering river, buzzards wheeling on thermals above the tiny, insignificant boats with their fishermen and their daps.

We arrived in two groups, an advance party and a pair of loiterers. The advance party had set up camp near the village at the westerly end of the loch; Matt and I arrived later, with sleeping-bags, rods, and ravaged clumps of six-packs loaded in the back of the MG. Glasgow must be the only city – perhaps apart from Dublin – where at least some off-licences are open at six in the morning.

The fish were in, but the loch was low, and the wind had

gusted gloomily and continually either from the north, or the north-east, or the south-east. Under these conditions 'the fish will not usually bite nor stir' – and nor had the sea trout of Loch Shiel. There had been, we were told, one monstrous swirl to the dap, and a brief weight of contact, but apart from that lucid moment, the days had passed with ennui and without incident. Our friends were listless; tempers had frayed quietly, and they were not happy campers. It had not been biting time. The weather had been dull and fair, grey day succeeding grey day; it had been bitterly, hip-chillingly cold at night ('the fish will not stir either for cold or fair weather'). We sat over soup, hip-flasks and stale sandwiches; our hearts sank.

For two days more we drifted the loch, dapped, dibbled, plumbed the depths with fast-sinking lines and sinking chins. A fish or two nodded at the flies, or boiled a foot down, following but not taking. Finally, a sea trout came and was solidly hooked on the Claret Bumble. It was a good fish, two pounds or more, which ran deep, behind the boat, the rod heavy with the contact. As the drogue was retrieved, it enveloped the fish, which promptly turned itself into slowly billowing nylon wings, and departed, leaving the hook in a cord. At that moment the drogue-rope undid itself from the thwart.

It is not easy playing a drogue. It is (I imagine) rather like playing a skate on a stick of liquorice: a pumping-action is all, and it is a slow business, as exciting as watching a carpet fade. Within reach of the boat, the leader parted. 'The twelve impediments. . . . The first, if your tackle is not good and well-made.' From the fifteenth-century list of disasters, the drogue should be instantly recognised as the missing eleventh Impediment.

The next day the weather turned, and with it came the rain, horizontal. We sat in tents and ate dry cheese biscuits. The mountain sides wore ribbons of white water. ('The seventh, if it rains.') The loch began to rise – and there we were, fishing the first few inches of extra water, when sea trout sometimes and salmon always move. But the river at Polloch had come down thick, bearing twigs, branches, peat-stain and carcases, the watershed exacting its price ('The fourth, if the water is very thick . . . from any flood recently fallen').

The following morning, dehydrated and hopeless after a whisky night of dancing, we fished from first light, and a small finnock took a point-fly suicidally, only to weed itself with juvenile decision in the long tresses of greenery that line the bed of the loch like streaming hair, where it runs out to the river. Again the wind rose in the cold of the early morning.

We fished on. A small brown trout was foul-hooked on a trailed spinner (and was eaten – a change from dry biscuits and viscous jam). We drifted downwind, further and further, prospecting along the shores, over the known lies. It was not, it had never been, biting time. A vast sea trout chased the skittering dap across the entrance to Polloch, showing its flank and blue, solid back; it came again to the wet-fly, following, following – until it saw the boat and swirled back into the blackness ('The third, if the fish are frightened by the sight of any man'). The wind rose again; a pair of black-throated divers and their melancholy cry flew out of earshot and to cover. We turned the boat into the wind on the oars, and roped the ancient Seagull.

The engine fired at the sixth attempt. The shear-pin snapped.

I still do not know what to recommend when you have spent hundreds of man-hours fishing the void of the black dog when conditions are against you, when you are tired and hungry and when you are faced with a six-mile row home into the teeth of squalls or great winds from any direction. Matt and I took an oar each, silently. The rod-tips, useless, dipped up and down beyond the stern at each oar-stroke. We did not even have the heart to trail a team of flies. We went stroke by stroke, the sick burble of the blade going in each time, muscle by muscle, mile by mile, with the slow pulse of water under the gunwales. Blisters bubbled and burst. Stroke by stroke, the broken rhythm of the blades repeating why-do-we-*do*-it-why-do-we-*do*-it-why-do-we-*do*-it.

The fourth limb, foully-furred, the limb that will give the black dog its full complement of legs, its stalking potential, is the final collapse of confidence. Another c-word. Two eyes; four legs. The creature slavers over your rod-hand, ready to raise its head and howl.

Confidence. Animals know. If you are afraid of dogs, real dogs, the fear is palpable. You will back away nervously from a small Yorkie. You will cross the road to avoid meeting an Alsatian. A neighbouring Dobermann would probably find you ringing the estate agent. No matter that these delightful canines' owners tell you that Bozo, Gnasher or Nipper, as they bare their gums and hurl their teeth at you, are 'only playing'. They know your anxiety, your abject confidence. Horses are the same: if you are afraid, they will mumble softly at your hand and then bite you as you offer them a Polo mint. Horses have big teeth and no gratitude. Pigs are scarcely different: if your fear disturbs them, they will try to eat you. Then, there are people: even the fearful maim those that fear more. Perhaps only the urban lives of the late twentieth-century could have invented 'Assertiveness Training'. The pity is that the race favours the strong. And the meek, say the appointment diaries and the Government statistics, shall not inherit the earth.

The confidence of a fisherman is a strange and difficult thing. I am not suggesting for a moment that fish somehow sense our weaknesses. Nor do I know anyone who is actually frightened of trout or salmon, although I can think of one or two pike that might threaten a tender constitution. But the fact remains that many of us go fishing to escape from the telephone, the love affair, the word-processor, the shifts of routine, the changingness of days and the incessant mysteries of work. Yet we can never cut ourselves off from the recent past: everything we were yesterday, we are today and are still. Our worries come with us – the bad letter, the overdraft, the betrayal. So, of course, do the luckier and more blessed of small events – the good photograph, the telling one-liner, the recovery and the congratulations. But it is often at the most troublesome of times that fishing becomes a craving, a coming up for air, a movement to a source and its haunting, absorbed moments of concentration and awareness. If I speak for myself, I know with certainty that if I bring anxiety or trouble with me from home, family or work I will fish badly, and the bag will be light or empty. Angling then does not heal a mind and does not mend a mood.

This tension, fighting itself into enervation and standstill, this inability to concentrate, does erode confidence. This shows up nowhere better than in the ways in which fish are lost. It is not that one's mechanical ability is affected: the cast is still relatively true, the fly floats lightly, no more mistakes are made than normal. But the first fish comes, a solid take, and the strike will be an instant too soon or too late. A second fish moves smartly to the surface-film nymph, and again, the hand's timing is wrong. A soft swear-word offends the beginning of the day. And so it continues.

The specific ways in which fish are lost during the play are of interest here. Commonly, a fish is hooked, apparently firmly, when after a second or two, and two or three kicks of the rod, the line slackens. This can happen maddeningly often with the wet fly, and it can be a sign that the fish has not had time to turn away with the fly, and has been, therefore, hooked in the bony front of the mouth where barb-purchase is not so good. An answer of a sort – although the black dog is ranging about on the shore – is to fish with the rod-point higher, to give the trout time. Angling with the rod-point low is perhaps another symptom of anxiety; to feel the fish, that decisive tug, to make sure the rise is felt, often seems to be an objective. Yet on the wet fly, if the fish is felt as it moves to the artificial then the angler will react, must react, inappropriately. A snatch replaces a smooth tightening.

Then there are the fish which come adrift halfway or more through the game. In my limited experience of big trout, it is exactly the biggest trout, the very biggest trout which are lost this way (were it not for the fact that 'no man can lose what he never had'). One problem may be that of hook-design. A hook with a narrow gape is a useless hook, suitable only for skimmer roach on a silent canal. It will not hold a big trout running hard. Nor will a hook soft in the wire. I also sometimes think that an over-sharpened hook can, as it were, slit too slightly across the gristle rather than embed in it, although I have no empirical data for believing this. Another reason why these big fish are lost is also, perhaps, that they are played too lightly. If the fight lasts through minutes, quarter-hours, then there is all the more time for the hook to work itself loose from whatever purchase it has gained. Again, nerves and anxiety are the culprits: the anxiety is avid to land the fish, the nerves are afraid of losing it. 'Must take this one – mustn't lose it.' But again, and for the same reasons, it is possible to fall into the opposite trap, to play fish too hard and with the rod too low, which exerts the maximum strain on the fish, but also on the hook-hold. The line must run between brutality and deference – a kind of strong tact of giving and retrieving, of pressure using itself knowingly.

Finally, there are landing-nets, and landing procedures. 'Lost at the net' is a phrase straight out of the Black Dog Dictionary of Angling Clichés, but it is a frequent occurrence: the hold giving way with an inaudible ping at the *moment juste* as the rod is raised; the point-fly caught in the net; the dropper(s) caught in the net; the trout cartwheeling away from the rim. Once more, anxiety makes haste, a bungling rush. Nothing should ever happen quickly at these tense moments. Yet, after three, four or more lost trout you are tempted to net the next before its proper time, are clumsy with the rod, your head flushed with excitement. There is a quick flurry of noise, a subsiding absence, and another trout is gone. The black dog shakes its body in delight.

I have pretended to solutions, to answers – I know none. As fish after fish is pricked, lost, put down, as confidence (that most curious and necessary attribute) leaks away into blank days, weeks and even seasons, it seems impossible that fish will ever again lie glistening and weighty on the shingle or as that satisfactory, final bowed weight in the net.

Every dog has its day, and the black dog has too many. But perhaps after all there is a kind of answer. These days, when the black dog mars my fishing or thinking of fishing, I don't fish. I wait, in the cool green of different valleys, or on the distant shores where the birds pass across the sky in energy and delight. There is the water, and its low, gentle sound; they are bringing down the ewes from the intake for shearing; flotsam from last winter's floods dries among the trees; and there, in a vivid line aimed upriver, there, van- ishing, is the kingfisher. It is all I have come to inherit, a rare repose. There will be time, and time enough. Out of turbulence and strain I have come fishing, and the trout will rise, soon or in some part of later. Sitting on into a cooler anticipation, I turn my face to the sun or the coming moon, and the black dog trembles like a heat-wave and dis- appears into its own reflection. In the waiting time, I begin to learn again some old, peaceful and very wise advice: study to be quiet.

CHAPTER SEVEN

The Children of the River

*T*he thin needle-line of the leader lies across the
mirror of the sky, drifting slowly into the good part
of the pool where the water is four and more feet
deep. I gather fly-line into my left hand, keeping a quiet
contact through the coils, all the time watching the leader,
which runs like a filament across the white liquid of an eye.
An autumn wind hisses in the branches of the beeches, and
a few late leaves struggle over the pool. Suddenly the line
tip dips, and instantly the rod goes up, meeting the contact,
then kicking under the weight of a fish that has taken deep.
I work the fish towards me, run a hand down the leader,
and click out the barbless hook from the top of the
grayling's jaw. The fish rights itself in the thin water at the
pool tail by my green waders, pauses an instant with a flex
of its black and crimson dorsal fin, then arrows off under a
weed-bed a yard or two away. The sun dwindles into the
far trees, a cold grey ball hazed in a mist that has lasted all
day and will last into the evening, gathering itself over the
Vale of York, shrouding the dipped beams of traffic going

home for the sports' results and Saturday tea. In this last hour of light, the grayling have started to forage for shrimp in the bottom gravels, and there's the chance of a better fish from among the scattering of heavy specimens at the head of the shoal. I check the leaded fly, then work out a yard or two of line, side-casting under low branches. The leader sets again onto the mirror of the pool, drifting slowly. . . .

Grayling have been good to me. They have saved poor seasons, and bad, tattered days in September when the birds are flocking onto the telephone wires through a raw and wind-battered afternoon. More importantly, perhaps, they have exercised my imagination, these fish of the Arctic. I think of them as wild, exiled from their historically proper habitat of karst and ice-bound tundra, their shoals now lost in a crowded England, far from home.

Of course theirs has been a successful exile. Where a river suits them – chalk water, or the downstream reaches of rainfed streams where water plants and silt are established – they breed spectacularly well. For this reason, the species still needs its apologists. Some trout fishers (Skues was one) loathe the grayling as much as I love them, because they believe that grayling colonise a river at the expense of trout. This has never been conclusively proved, and is in fact unlikely. Grayling spawn at a different season, and characteristically lie in different parts of the stream, and therefore competition between the two species is, to some extent, naturally controlled.

I learned my grayling fishing with Owen on the Wharfe. The late Reg Righyni's book (*Grayling*. London, 1968) was our touchstone and, although I would now dispute one or two of the grand old man's dicta, I still think it is one of the best of all grayling books in a thin literature. Perhaps only T.K. Wilson understood the Dales rivers better.

The Wharfe lent me my first big catches of grayling (a big catch then was, say, eight fish) and most of them came from the pools around Grassington, though I also fished at Bolton Abbey, Addingham, Arthington and Pool. It was in these places that I began to understand the peculiar attractions of grayling fishing: days in October when the leaves have been tumbling in nut-and-russet windflukes and the fish have been coming on an Orange Partridge; or black days in December when the float has swooped unerringly beneath the smooth, cold waters. Best of all, the grayling were forgiving to a newcomer, particularly after the first frosts had keened their appetites, and they were also very beautiful. On the Wharfe, black shades to gunmetal grey to silver; the fish in your hands has scales that look as though they had been newly struck in some underwater foundry.

When I think of a fishing river, a trout and grayling river, I almost invariably think and dream of the Wharfe. It was the first river (as distinct from a beck) I ever fished seriously with a fly – more properly, with three flies, all classic Yorkshire spiders – and I have continued to fish it all the seasons long, in high water and low, through joy and disappointment. I have covered it with a dry fly where it begins as a jumpable rush at Beckermonds, girt by rocks, each tiny pool holding one or more swift-taking trout (some of them larger than you think). I have knelt at Kilnsey – deep, stiff-limbed genuflections to the spring olives as the fish begin to form up under the banks to the trickle of wind-driven naturals. I have waded the deeper pools down at Bolton Abbey, roll-casting with the big, easy-actioned rod, watching the long bow in the line straighten quickly as a trout has taken the point-fly at the end of its travel. At Addingham, and Burley, and Pool, where the waters widen and the river is barbel-sized, riven by weirs and backed-up, never-ending slownesses, I have either cast a fly, or put up the long-trotting rod, in the summers and autumns of a boy's clear weather.

The Wharfe in many ways is a paradigm river, falling into clearly-defined areas or regions that the zoologists might call 'trout zone', 'grayling zone', 'coarse fish zone' and so on. The headwaters gather from Cam Fell – now, alas, with its forestry plantings – and the infant river then runs rushing, if it runs overground, through the upland Norse country of scree and limestone scarp through Becker-monds, Deepdale, Yockenthwaite and Hubberholme, the last with its fine medieval church whose 'Mouseman' furniture is a great delight (I was once told to go away and count the mice carved into the pews when I was being a more than usually tedious little boy). Then at Kilnsey, where the Wharfe gathers the Black Keld and the Skirfare (whose Norse name means literally 'bright-flowing'), the river widens over rock terraces, and slows into the expanses of proper pools where you will find fish smutting every day in all the hot Augusts. This is still classic rainfed trout water, but one gets the first real hint of grayling towards the bottom end of the Kilnsey reach, where the Wharfe turns through Grass Wood, that botanist's paradise of fern and orchid and other rare flowers whose names I don't know, although Bill would. From here, and down through Grassington and Linton to Appletreewick ('Ap'trick'), Burnsall, Barden and the whole lower river, there are – there used to be – good grayling stretches, where weed and silt are long established and where the grayling find the slacker, slowly-gliding runs that are so much to their liking. I think particularly of Kennedy's Dub, that whirling deep that runs for a hundred yards and more by Linton Church; or the bend by the sewage works at the bottom of the Grassington water, where we once found the grayling working a hatch of needles one mild October; or the pools between the Cavendish Pavilion and Bolton Priory, where you fish loops of the river below the massive tracery of ruined stone reaching upwards into the autumn mist. Here is the mellow country of superstition and the Green Man, where unknown footsteps follow you gently through the dusk as you walk back from the river in the gathered twilight where darkness folds over villages. Below this, through Addingham and Ilkley and Pool, coarse fish begin to establish themselves. There are dace, and chub; and lower still, where the river spreads itself generously into long, still reaches where light gathers over the flat lands, at Tadcaster and Ulleskelf, there are barbel. Even here, though, where patient men sit under green umbrellas and daub their hooks with arcane concoctions of luncheon meat and sweetcorn, even here I like to think that the Wharfe carries some water-memory of its beginnings in the steep dale, of turbulence, limestone and the brawl of oxygenated water clattering among the rocks, haunted by dippers and the mad cries of sandpipers.

When I say we learned our grayling fishing on the Wharfe, I mean that we had to learn to fish specifically for grayling, rather than casting a downstream wet fly at a venture – what is sometimes described, tautologously, as 'fishing the water'. To succeed with grayling on these rivers, you must think of the species in unaccustomed ways. Grayling don't often lie in the same kind of water as do trout, for example. You will never find them (or very seldom find them) intercepting a hatch of fly in the quick water at the head of a pool; these are places favoured by trout, at least in October and early November before the trout have run upstream or otherwise withdrawn to spawn and become torpid. You will typically find grayling in the glides and flats, as the river begins to thin towards the draws of pool tails. You will sometimes find them in the real deeps, waters of weight and fathom-darkness, scours by huge glacial boulders or mysterious blacknesses under a high bank and age-old overhanging trees, places where you cannot see the bottom even with the river at mid-summer low. Occasionally, in the run-off from an autumn flood, with the river running vaguely coloured, you will find grayling at the very edges of the stream, in water only inches deep, or in foam-circling slacks off the rush of the river between one pool and the next.

One also has to learn – it took me long enough, and maybe I never did – that the fish react to the fly in ways different from trout. Grayling lie deep, usually if not invariably on the bottom. I have never seen them lie in midwater (although other anglers have reported them behaving in this way). When there is no autumn hatch to stimulate their greed, they will seldom come willingly to a fly presented at the surface. You must therefore fish deep, with tiny weighted flies. When the hatch begins – and grayling will usually respond to any kind of hatch – they rise to the fly from the bottom, taking each one with a kind of quick, downward-turning swirl. They do not sip austerely, like aldermanic trout, or blunder excitedly after a floating artificial before it has the chance to escape. They are altogether more rapid and eager. Perhaps, also, they are less discerning and more tolerant fish than their celebrated summer relatives. In some ways, I would quibble with Francis Francis's description, 'lady of the stream'; I think of grayling as the children of the river, clustered, enthusiastic, restless, always rather hungry. But like children, they can also be sullen, and sulk all day until sundown. Leaf-fall in continued low water can sicken them. Snow-broth, too, I think, can suppress their spirits. Pollution of any kind is damaging enough to be fatal to whole populations: we should never forget that the grayling are Arctic fish of cold, clear and utterly pure flowing water; they will vanish from rivers that become even remotely dirty.

I look back over what I have written here and see that this has, perhaps, been a chronicle of loss, a book of vanishings. On the Wharfe, as on many of the Dales rivers, the grayling are slowly, even if almost imperceptibly, disappearing. They are not yet altogether gone – in places, they still seem abundant – and there is yet at least some hope. But I doubt if I will ever again see grayling, as I once did, as far up the river as Buckden. Even in the places where they were once most numerous, the shoals have dwindled in size, and critically, there seem fewer juveniles in each shoal. Gravel-workings on the upper and middle river cannot have done good. Millions of gallons of water are now abstracted from the lower reaches. Nor, to my inauspicious eye, is the Wharfe as clean as it once was. In summer's low water, the once-bright stones under your feet are unnaturally slimy with brown and filamentous algae, creeping over the thin water like a dying stain. Some clubs on the middle and lower river no longer issue tickets for grayling fishing; others operate mandatory catch-and-release policies in order to conserve the stocks. I wish them well, and the signs may be encouraging. Nevertheless, the grayling, particularly the little fish, are virtually gone from the first wall-end above Grassington Bridge, and other sure haunts. In the poor hatches of October needles, where once you could be almost certain of a fish or two in the last half-hour of light, you will fish on into the cold falling across the fields, and turn for home disappointed and puzzled, remembering the diary entries of fifteen and more years ago. Your fishing begins to become a continual reminiscence, stalked by a sense of misdirection, unease and blame.

If I was apprenticed on the Wharfe, then later, at university in Newcastle, I began to fish the Border rivers for grayling, rivers so prestigious that their names don't even carry definite articles. One doesn't fish The Tweed or The Teviot; they are Tweed and Teviot always, mighty and serious names. They were, and happily still are, remarkable grayling rivers. Fishing them also introduced me to a remarkable man: Don Gibson.

Looking back, I see that there have been several magnificent fishermen here. I have been lucky to fish with them. Gibson, however, was unique (I use the past tense because Don moved many years ago to Canada to design ice-breakers for their navy, and sadly we have lost contact). His marks for tidiness, apparent thought, and presentation would certainly have been in the 'could do better' class. Yet, he never went fishing without what is called luck. But, since fishing holds a mirror to our moods and lives, we know at root (and uncomfortably) that luck makes itself. Don could catch fish in roadside puddles – and probably did, when no one was looking. I never saw him without my spirits lifting, and only belatedly did I realise that Don had something that most of us struggle all the years long to find, something close to genius.

His car at the time was an elderly Renault held together by bits of cardboard and Sellotape. In a mild mood, he called it Frog, and kicked it reflectively. Frog responded by 'Being Temperamental'.

One bitter autumn day, after meeting hungover and late by the Arches, we drove from Newcastle towards Jedburgh, leaving hot oil on the road behind us. Frog's head-gasket had blown. Don suspected the car of a deliberate act of angling sabotage. For Frog, the journey became a penitential hop from one garage to another, from one can of Castrol to the next. Lurching over Carter Bar, the inside of the car gradually filled up with acrid smoke, from where engine oil had spilt onto the exhaust manifold and boiled itself away into a sticky mess of hot tar that quickly became a choking and viscous vapour. Don pushed back the sunroof and began to hum, and then, as a born Scot, went into tone-deaf peals of 'Scotland the Brave' as we crossed the border. Any sensible chap would have called the recovery services, written off the day's fishing, and gone early to the nearest bar. I still had much to learn.

When things became critical in the garageless snows of the high Cheviots, Don stopped. He cast around on Frog's bottom for the bit of cardboard box that was doing service for the floor. Then he took the top off the engine, removed the old gasket, and made a new one from the cardboard, cutting out the template with his fishing knife. I see his face now, vivid with blue cold, leering happily at me from twisted metal and snowdrift. He was a wonderful, if unorthodox, engineer. Given the chance, I expect Don could have adjusted a grayling's fins and made it fly.

The first time we went after grayling together I made the mistake of being effortlessly condescending. Had I not fished the Dales? Indeed I had. And had I not read Righyni's book? Quite spuriously I thought I knew something about grayling fishing. I explained, in superior tones that make me blanch now, where the fish would lie, what they would take, the kind of tackle to use. We were trotting brandlings on Teviot, and the river was frost-bound, low, and clear. 2lb line would be about right, I said, and a size 18 hook. We could expect, I intoned, fish up to about a pound. They would have shoaled up at this time of year, etc. The etceteras, equally, took much time in a telling as portentous as it proved useless.

Don was nothing if not surprising. I have seen him take trout, in a flat calm on the lake, with a size 2 dapping fly fished from a 16-foot dapping rod. I have seen him dap upwind – for us, an impossibility, for Don, a deliberate minor tactic. For those Teviot grayling, those creatures of ethereal finesse and the quick, light hand, he tackled up with a Mark IV carp rod, 6lb line straight through to a size 10 hook, and two big lobworms. I shook my head ruefully at him, and gave out some poor crack about fishing for pollack. It made no difference.

We started fishing about a hundred yards apart in a long, steady glide. Conditions were good: the ground under our wader-studs was stiff with overnight frost, and a big moon paled in the blue sky, a fading grapefruit suspended in a washed clarity.

Twenty minutes later there was a whistle from upstream. I looked round to see Don's carp rod bending stiffly. Silly beggar, I thought, he's probably hooked a small trout by the tail. (This had happened before.) The whistling became more urgent. My thoughts turned uncharitably to salmon kelts, but I came grumbling out of the water and walked up to where Don was smoking a second cigarette while the Mark IV had taken on the curve for which it had been designed. I looked over his shoulder into the green, lucid water and my smug face froze. A couple of minutes later and the fish was lying in the net on the frosty grass. It weighed 2lb 3oz. His first grayling.

As an historical aside, I ought to say that at that time the

British grayling record had just been thrown open, with the qualifying weight for entries at the magic specimen figure of 2lb. I suspect, although I cannot prove, that Don's first grayling would have been the first, albeit short-lived, British record. It was an entirely typical bit of Gibsonism.

Around lunchtime we were fishing a pool called the Sandbeds. Don had started in at the head, in what I thought was unsuitable water, only a foot deep. Concentrate on the dubs and holes at this time of year, I'd said to him knowingly. But Don, singing badly again, swam his bunch of serpents around in a slack off the current. Even his silhouette suggested the best, crude, totally willing kind of hope – a boy's hope. Then came the second whistle. I looked upstream into the light, and cursed. But cursing did no good; it only seemed to encourage him.

Don's second grayling weighed exactly the same as the first. He grinned. I thought you said a pound grayling was a good one, he said. That the fish shoal up in deep dubs at this time of year. That you couldn't use nylon over 2lb or a hook bigger than a size 16. That lobworms were too big a bait.

It was a delightful and chastening day. Gibson must be the only man in the world who has opened his account with the grayling with a brace of 2lb specimens. Meanwhile, I had hooked many leaves and turned an interesting shade of purple.

Teviot and Tweed gave us some marvellous fishing during the winters. Tweed, particularly, was full of problems and promise. It was easy to imagine 3 and 4lb grayling in those wide, deep, inaccessible and underfished pools in the lower river. Probably those fish, or their progeny, are there still – all my plans with a link-leger came to nothing – and will surprise someone some winter's day when the light is closing in.

I had a strange day on Tweed in the winter of 1981, fishing the Junction at Kelso. It was an experience out of Pritt, say, or Walbran, a day of sharp frost and ice and landing-nets frozen into large art deco jars, or shapes trans-lucent as flawed, inverted lampshades. That is not to suggest that frost, ice and grayling always go together. I think the best conditions for grayling fishing in midwinter are a relatively warm daytime air temperature after a night frost, and a water that has a cold translucence about it – a water neither too high nor too turbid, and one not carrying snow-melt, which certainly deters the fish. However, on the day we arrived at Kelso, having travelled cautiously over slippery but just-passable roads through Carter Bar and the high moors, Tweed was entirely frozen over below the bridge. Great rafts of ice (locally known as 'grue') were grating and grinding, their surface edges catching the low winter sun. The Junction, one of the best grayling pools on the river, and the one we had intended to fish, was choked with slowly-moving floes, with the merest channels of open water between them. There were several feet of ice at the edge of the river, and despite the wan sun, the temper-ature was still below freezing. Watching the river from the bridge, we knew the feeling of hostile beauty that comes in deepest midwinter from a northern landscape. The ice at the river's edge was flocked with frozen feathers.

One of the things I love about fishing is the benignity and knowledge of strangers. The man at Dickson's tackle shop, for instance, where we bought tickets, was openly enthusiastic. 'If ye can live wi' the grue ye'll be OK,' he said. 'They were doon las' Tuesday, and they'd eight.' I won-dered where 'they', the fabled grayling fishers of Tweed, had found space to cast their lines among the floes, let alone how they had managed to play and land grayling through the ice. We bought hot bridies, and fished anyway.

We began, clumsy and numb, the cold biting at our faces. Nothing happened for a long time – just the ice implacably churning, and the occasional shocking thrash as a kelt came out between the floes. Only limited casting and retrieving were possible, since the line froze in the rings. Periodically, we sucked ice away from the end tackle –

'loving the rod', as Graham MacGregor put it later. The trick was to keep a given length of line beyond the rod, and to keep the tip high; the nylon would otherwise freeze into a thin ice-needle within minutes. But we needed no reminding how bad conditions were. The brandlings were freezing on our hooks. (Old Yorkshire Fishermen, on these occasions, used to suck worms, suck maggots to salivate them warmly into liveliness before impaling them. When and if I qualify as an Old Yorkshire Fisherman, I will do the same. But not before then.)

About midday, the sun became a stronger smear. This made fishing not exactly pleasant, but at least bearable. The ice opened up a little. The orange blob of the float was easier to see as it wound its insignificant way through the ice. Banking on the reputation of the Junction Pool, we carried on fishing. A local angler, spending his lunch-break by the river, gave us much useful advice, and his confidence was infectious. Immediately after he left, the float slid away beneath the river. And again. Before long we were looking at two fine grayling of about a pound-and-a-half apiece. There was, given the conditions, no chance of playing the fish. The pool was choked with grue and there was twelve feet of ice at the water's edge. All we could do was keep the rod high, maintain pressure, and steer the hooked grayling between the floes, finally pulling them across the ice to our feet in a way that resembled the beaching of salmon. Our only attempt to lead fish downstream to where they could be netted resulted in a landing-net which, in Arthur Ransome's words, had 'turned into a glass bucket, very beautiful to look at but useless for landing-fish' (*Rod and line*, 1929).

It was never going to be a day for numbers of grayling. In all we managed to take, I think, seven. The best were all around the pound-and-a-half mark. We had lost others at the edge of the ice, and the greatest activity had come in the two hours following lunch, before the air turned arctic again and the ice closed in once more.

As we left, we turned on the bridge to look back at Tweed, the water a reddened greyness after the setting sun. A solitary kelt smashed its way out of the river it was leaving. The huge floes cracked and groaned and rasped. It was an apocalyptic and a dead vision, turning to a mono-chrome intensity as the sun sank towards the year's deep midnight. But no, perhaps it was not John Donne; it was like fishing for grayling in the pages of Dante, some frozen, purgatorial circle that fishermen might be burnished in, for joy and punishment.

We adapt ourselves to opportunity. It is now many years since I have fished these streams regularly or seriously for grayling, and I realise now how much I miss their almost unexpected charms, the water's irregular hiss among the rocks between pools, the line drawing in your hands as the current weighs again, or the float dipping. . . . Yes, the float, its red-orange, hand-painted lentil top above its wire stem a token of contact with all you seek to find, riding the dark glides; and then the pause at the end of the swim, where you check line and see the float hover back, and imagine the bait rising gently, enticingly in the water. Then you strike on the off-chance – a good, bold, rod-sweeping affair to take up the slack quickly from tens of yards of line. There, at last, surprised again, you feel the kick and drag on the rod as, downstream of you and altogether invisible, a grayling begins to kite and gyrate, deep in the flow. You bring the fish towards you with the rod high, winding to maintain the pressure, keeping your hands gentle and the play light. Finally, you see the grayling's dorsal fin flag at the surface, erected against the pull from the rod as the fish tries, weakly now, to skew again in the winter river. Then, as you unhook the fish with as much deftness as the cold will allow, it feels almost as if you have understood a problem or a mystery, and made each become a palpable kind of riddle whose solution lay all the time in the mind informing the speed and fine dexterity of your own hands. Suddenly, all the abstract connections make sense – or seem to – and are realised in the slow shock of the line, tight, connected, to the actual, living creature now to be released from the green folds of the landing-net. Somewhere here, also, in this grey, cold and quiet country, is the fleeting sense of happiness.

These days it is chalk water that flows in my head, a lush clarity of gravel and weed-bed caught under a wide sky. Again, I know that I have been lucky to fish on one or more of these streams, streams where, with absorbed delight, you can watch the grayling haunting the river-bed in slow shadows, in easy shoals under the long slant of autumn sunlight.

It is a very different kind of grayling fishing, a form of stalking, every stone and every movement visible. It is also totally instructive. The little grayling, for instance, are almost always active, flicking themselves from the bottom to investigate any bit of nothing floating over them. The middle-sized fish lie more quietly, usually rather deeper; they begin to move when there is sufficient fly, and then feed earnestly, for two hours or more into the twilight. Then you will catch them on small spider patterns and, as the light fails, on weighted nymphs. The bigger fish, on the other hand, lie in the deepest dubs, solitary, or in small groups of two or three. You will need a heavily-weighted fly for them, and a quick hand after the draw of the deep fly has induced a take.

I carry one memory above all with me from the grayling of the chalk. It is not a memory of particularly big fish, but of small fish and a poor day, when the grayling had seemed altogether sullen. The wind rasped on the telephone wires; lips chapped and hands cramped in the cold; the weighted flies – Killer Bug, Shrimp, usually so successful – had done nothing, and there was no further inspiration in the flybox. Grey clouds fled under the higher pall of an autumn front. Birds too were utterly silent. There was only the wind, the smell of earth from the ploughing, the fractured sky and the afternoon dwindling.

In the last half hour of light the grayling began to move. They were not moving to fly, but tailing for shrimp and hoglice. I could watch a ring, another ring, caused by a grayling's tail as the fish itself tipped its snout into the gravel. Stooping to catch silhouettes in the grey glaze of the pool tail, soon I saw two fish, then three, then four, all tailing hard. Then I began to cast at these ghosts, these fleet shadows of the day's end. It was becoming too dark to see properly, the wind continued its restless applause in the trees, and I cast and struck only by instinct as the grayling continued to forage. It was instinct, evanescence, the hints of contact prompting the wrist's quick turn, the line's weight and tautness as the iron went in.

I took three of those fish – fish at the very end of a washed-out day in late autumn when the year seems tired – but it was not the capture that stayed with me. It was the final image: the afternoon steepening early into night, the lacquer of the pool tail, and within that, the fish tailing, minutely disturbing the thin water. It was almost as if I had stumbled on and into another time, displaced, surprised, as if I were only some fragment in the scene and had almost dissolved into it.

The flat lands; the biting wind; the afternoons decaying into the darkness; and those children of the river, the grayling. Always in the mind's own quietness, that other country still exists, living most vividly just on the edge of sleep.

CHAPTER EIGHT
The Reading of Rod and Line

Perhaps it is almost over, this journey among shadows, among the lost figures, the men, the fish, the tides. Perhaps none of it was altogether true. Perhaps this is already the concrete future, spent with radioactivity and drought. Perhaps, again, it is all beginning.

I have come far enough – far enough to know that I have ended more or less where I began, with trout and running water. A hundred yards from where I sit, a beck runs brim full at the bottom of the valley, and I know that tonight the fish will be rising on and on into the darkness to a small sedge. (If I put on my long-abandoned entomologist's face I could tell you that the sedge are *Anabolia nervosa* . . . but to you and me they are small brown sedges, wisps, wisheens, whispers of wings among the bushes.) And tomorrow I could take you to my other river, a wider place among the scarps and uplands of the north, a water of rock-ledges and tree-light where you would fish all day, cunning, contriving, to take two or three wild browns. If you have been raised on small stillwaters and their stocked rainbows you might not find the fishing worth your while (although I certainly hope you would) – but there are wine-glasses in the fishing hut, and we could sit for an hour with a bottle cooled by the stream, and watch the uncatchable fish rising while we drank, glimpsing the martins out of the corners of our eyes. Perhaps there will be the kingfisher; perhaps not.

It is not that I came to this deliberately. I did not set out to meet this with any particular purpose or with some final set of principles in mind. Taught by haphazard and the genius of chance, this future somehow met me. And yet I also know that one of the things that has disciplined my own thinking about fishing has been the literature of the pastime. Eclectic, humorous, often bizarre with the eccentricity of loneliness, but more often wise with imagination and hope, writings on fish and fishing absorb me, loaded as they are with memories and trouble, rods and dreams.

Like many fishermen I know, I do not read primarily for instruction. Instruction there is in plenty: how to stalk trout, how to play trout, how to tie up patterns from arcane materials that might tempt trout. . . . All this, and more, one can read in the (usually much-used) fishing shelves of any public library and in the pages of any of the numerous fly-fishing periodicals. And it is not, of course, that I am above and beyond instruction; on many occasions by the water, I am much in need of it, I think, as I watch the fly catch the leader once again on its forward travel, or as I unravel yet another wind-knot with the eye-defying needle. Yet if I need instruction, I need other things from the literature more. I need what I most lack: a sense of connection and responsibility; a sense of place and permanence; the foster-ing of discrimination and the tact of delight. Bound up with these things, there is too the sense of time passing: the book in your hands, the travel of the eye across the page, the medium and the message, are where the past and the future meet.

What can reading give us that practical experience

cannot? First, reading can supply us with a useful corrective focus. Perhaps we tend to think we are too much unique, caught in our difficult present with its noise, hurry and expensive gadgetry, its worries and its tackle-shop credit accounts. The fly patterns in our hi-tech boxes are, we surely feel, a huge improvement on those tied generations ago; our space-age rods, light, dangerous, are likewise more productive implements than the greenheart and the spliced built cane of our grandfathers and the hollowed willow or ashplant of three centuries ago; our approach to the water, the selection of the fly or flies, the feathered cast ending in chemically-treated double-strength nylon, are governed by what seem like rapid and definitive advances in understanding. The fishing industry that surrounds us would have it so; the recent literature, the advertisements, the casting clinics and demonstrations – all conspire to give us, in our present, the illusion of being somehow privileged and gifted, the inheritors of Progress.

The literature of the past, however, suggests otherwise, and it should be neither dismissed nor neglected. For some, of course, 'the past' is a kind of remote illusion, a dark backward and abysm of time peopled by scrawls and children and untellable mouths whose voices were unrecognisable. But we are nearer, much nearer to those voices than we think.

Try a small experiment. Say one generation is twenty-five years. Four people, therefore, represent one hundred years. Now imagine those four people stretched back in time, hands outstretched and linked. The furthest outstretched hand will reach into the end of the last century. Add another four people, and you will have reached beyond the invention of the dry fly. Add another four, and the furthest outstretched hand will almost touch Charles Cotton. Add another four, and you will have spanned almost all extant fishing literature. Add another four, and you will be able to hold a text of the *Treatise*, newly sent from Wynkyn de Worde's press in Fleet Street.

Now imagine twenty people in a room, in the train, in a queue for the last bus. Twenty people – a small and motley crew. There are probably more in your fishing club or syndicate. And yet, hands linked and stretched back into the supposedly remote, difficult and illusory past, those twenty people will span five centuries. Twenty people only, then, stand between you and the beginning of all fishing literature in this country. 'The past' is closer than our sense of late 20th century psychosis cares to imagine.

In its literature, too, there are the same concerns, the same intimacies and moments of excitement and disconsolation. When, for example, Dame Juliana's anonymous sleeve left the page, fishing had been – must have been – a sporting pastime of the English (more properly, the Anglo-French) nobility for perhaps two hundred years. It is a literature already rich in wisdom, already carrying the viral, vital enthusiasms of its own past. Even at this relatively early date, for instance, there was more to fishing than the mere catching of fish: even if the angler catches no fish, writes the anonymous Dame, or even if he loses a fish, 'then at the very least he shall have his wholesome and pleasant walk, and have a sweet savour of various plants and flowers that will make him hungry. . . . He will hear the melodies of the harmony of birds . . .' And so on. Which is not of course to say that medieval anglers lived swooning among nature by the waterside; like their after-comers in the running centuries, they too were preoccupied with catching fish, and the advice given in the *Treatise* sounds almost contemporary: 'And for the principal point of angling, keep yourself always away from the water and the fish's sight – back on the land or behind a bush or tree – so that the fish does not see you. For if he does, he will not bite'. And further: 'take care that you do not shadow the water any more than you can help, for that is a thing which will frighten the fish, and if he is frightened, he will not bite for a good while afterward'.

Or again, on the timing of the strike: 'do not be too hasty

108

to smite him, nor too late. . . . And see that you do not over-smite the strength of your line, lest you break it'. Amen.

Or again, on weather: 'from the beginning of May until September . . . the biting time is early in the morning from four o'clock until eight; in the afternoon, from four until eight, but this is not so good as in the morning. And if there is a cold, whistling wind and it be a dark, lowering day, then the fish will usually bite all day. . . . And if you see the trout or the grayling leap at any time of the day, angle to him with a dub [a fly] appropriate to that same month . . .' In other words, fish the morning or the evening rise (or both), and pay special attention to moving fish.

And on the autopsy: 'for baits for great fish, keep especially to this rule: when you have taken a great fish, open up the belly, and whatever you find in it, make that your bait, for it is best'. One thinks of Skues and his baby-plate, and a thousand late-night inspections in a sink's white saucers. Aligned with this, there is too the advice of the 17th century Robert Venables, in his incomparable *The Experienced Angler.* 'When you come first to the river in the morning, with your rod beat upon the bushes or boughs which hang over the water, and by their falling upon the water you will see what sorts of flies are there in greatest numbers. . . .' To which I would only add, look too for night-fallen midges in the spiders' webs in the rafters of the hut or boat-house, and look on the summer's dawn-drying rocks for the shucks of sedges and stone-fly. And think to yourself *the thing that hath been, it is that which shall be; and that which is done is that which shall be done: and there is no new thing under the sun.* A huge inter-connectedness runs through the literature: as you stoop to examine the marrow-spoon, as you drift your flies over the place where the last fish rose, as you watch the mayflies struggling from their nymphal skins on the slick of a bay of a becalmed Irish lough, remember also that others, many and greater, have also stooped and drifted and watched, and that your intrigued and local actions were also theirs. You are no longer solitary, however you garb yourself in the metaphor of solitary hunter; you are both a continuation and a new beginning. And continuity brings its own responsibilities. That is one useful corrective focus that reading can bring.

Linked with this, and a second thing that reading can give us, is a sense – an enhanced sense – of community. Again, this abuts onto our sense (perhaps, after all, it is only my sense) of unique privilege and solitariness. Solitariness there is, but it is continually modified by dialogue with both the quick and the dead, and with the rules and principles (I suppose, once again, the ethics) of fishing as they have developed across the centuries. Which is no more than to say that humans are inescapably dialectic, caught in the tensions of past and future, effective and ineffective, good and bad, language and silence. That dialectic is inscribed into the individual psyche, as, perhaps, is the will to resolve its tensions. But it may also be the case that such a dialectic is also inscribed into the history of the past itself, as evidenced in the literature. Every system of knowledge, after all – and who doubts that fishing literature encodes a system of knowledge? – carries within it its own genesis and its own potential for growth. A useful analogy may be made with evolutionary theory: slice through a 20th century tree and you will find its history written concentrically within the trunk; inspect a salmon's scale and you will find sea-winters and summer spawnings, time past in time present. Knowledge systems, languages, literature, may also (I think) behave in the same perceptible and perceptual way: just as the *Treatise* carries the birth and subsequent history of the pastime with it, so Walton and Cotton are at least partly in dialogue with the *Treatise*, so Venables is in dialogue with Cotton . . . and so on. So, for that matter, is Skues in dialogue with Halford, and Sawyer with Skues, and Clarke with Ivens. History does not run through phases as a commuter train runs through stations; whatever it has been, it is still, however that may be modified in the structure of the present. The first growth-ring is still visible in the salmon's scale. *Is there any thing whereof it may be said, See, this is new? it hath been already of old time, which was before us.*

So, we have come to the sense of the individual, and the sense of community and history, and hinted that both are dialectic. But there is another point here, and it is this: the things and how-to of fishing can be known, but the nature, the essence, of fishing can never be known. That is, the rods, the flies, nets, tackle, implements are empirical objects, phenomenal things belonging to the world of appearances and experience. But behind this world of appearances, and implying it, is a darker, more difficult and spectral world, the noumenal world of 'things in themselves', 'things as they are'. Yet the nature of things as they are, the nature of essence, is unknowable; therefore the nature of fishing itself is unknowable. Defining the nature of fishing is in this sense impossibly ambitious; it is like attempting to define the nature of belief or the nature of God. Still, just as it is necessary to attempt to define the nature or the idea of God in order to give one a point of orientation and reference, so – and for much the same reasons – it is necessary to attempt to define the nature of fishing. It is perhaps the dialectic between appearance and essence which has spawned such a great reflective fishing literature.

As Immanuel Kant slips away silently but humanely cursing, and as Hegel sharpens his quill with a derisory smile on his lips, we are certainly in the meshes of a theoretical net. But the distinction between appearance and essence is not so hard to grasp. Think of fishing flies. Take, as an easy example, a Waterhen Bloa. Here it is on this sheet of paper: size 14 hook, primrose silk lightly dubbed with mole's fur, and a sparse hackle (two turns only) from the covert of a waterhen wing. This artefact, tied last winter, belongs to the world of appearances. But, on the other hand, it is an indefinite, not a definite, Waterhen: A

111

Waterhen, not The Waterhen. There are many other Waterhen Bloas – some tied on larger or smaller hooks, some tied with water-rat not mole, some tied with a bulky or overlong hackle, some on hooks blunted by stones on the back-cast. These Waterhens certainly resemble the scrap on the table; one might say, they partake of its nature. But the nature of the Waterhen Bloa itself does not belong to the world of appearance, but to the world of essence. And one cannot tie on an essential Waterhen and catch trout (except, perhaps, in heaven – and look where that left Mr Theodore Castwell).

If things in themselves cannot be known, then the nature of God, or fishing, or next door's cat cannot be known. All that leaves us with is contingency, will, hiatus and prejudice. This condition is what Hegel, in dialogue with Kant, called 'alienation', the separation of the individual consciousness from the noumenal world. (And it was, incidentally, out of separation of self from the nature of fishing that this book began – to find joy again.) The task here, then, is to reconcile self with community, and self with the nature of things, by which of course I mean the nature of fishing.

It is salutary to realise that as we spend time by the waterside we are participating in a set of natural processes which existed before us and whose ends and purposes are unknown to us. We ourselves are implied in the processes and purposes around us, but we cannot guess their ends any more than we can guess the outcomes of our own apparently most casual actions; nevertheless, we are included, *for that which befalleth the sons of men befalleth beasts; even one thing befalleth them: as the one dieth, so dieth the other; yea, they have all one breath.* To take an extreme and obvious example: say you are fishing an upland trout river where the fish run small. You will of course put back, using barbless hooks, much of what you catch. Consider what happens to that returned six-ouncer. In the autumn it will move upriver, past waterfall and flood and November's waterlogged, fallen branches, and assume the spawning redds along with other milt-ready males. Competitive, aggressive, it arches its back and opens its jaw wide at intruders. Eventually, its milt will mingle with the larger female's stream of eggs and the pair of fish will lie side by side, taut with exhausted energy, and life will begin again. But for life to have begun at all at this moment on this redd depends on your own casual hand-twist as you slipped the fish off the hook back in July, or April, or last year when, as little more than a parr, the troutling took your Black Gnat. You have been included; you are implicated in the scene; you have touched the future although you can never see its end. This inclusion is replicated every time you catch or release a fish, or stock from the tank behind the tractor, or construct a weir, or rake the spawning beds: our own local actions are less random and unimportant than we may think. *He hath made every thing beautiful in his time: also he hath set the world in their heart, so that no man can find out the work that God maketh from the beginning to the end.*

At the same time, though, we are reading, coming to know history, and community, and dialectic, taste and choice. The nature of fishing, composed of spirit, may be unknowable but it can come to consciousness in the developing awareness of human beings. But developing awareness can only be brought about by reflection; reading aids reflection. The reading self, that is, reconciles the abstract in the developed understanding of the present. Stories, instruction, a workable set of ethics. . . . all help us to explain ourselves to ourselves and to each other, and that attempt at explanation is – since we are inescapably dialectic – one of the prime requirements of being alive, and human. We may not catch fish, but we are able to say why we tried to catch them in the first place. Speculation is sometimes more powerful than Progress.

From abstraction and essence we have come to taste and discrimination; educating taste and discrimination means studying the literature of the past. That literature gives us access to communities with which we are able to identify, and principles to which we may (or may not) accede. Those principles include a framework of rules and duties – the ethics of fishing. Our knowledge of fishing's ethics, through literature and our own experience, bridges community and self, in the sense that if we are to continue as a member of the community of fishermen we must voluntarily accede to ethics which fulfil our own requirements as individuals seeking satisfaction from the apparent world around us. Our essential interests, as fishermen, of course include catching fish; but they also include far more than fish-catching: clean rivers; good spawning; conservation and management; the politics of hope. And so from abstraction and essence, through reading, the community and the individual, we have come to self-interest and the essentialism of the practical. That interpenetration, of self and community, is most clearly evident in fishing's literature. Reading is realisation; it helps to create our delight. *Wherefore I perceive that there is nothing better, than that a man should rejoice in his own works; for that is his portion: for who shall bring him to see what shall be after him?*

The sense of quiet delight. This is perhaps a third and final good of reading, and reveals itself both in the stories fishermen have told and in the language anglers have used to describe the central and peripheral features of their pastime. Those people reading this far will remember that I claimed earlier that knowledge-systems carried their own histories with them. Reading the literature of fishing also means gaining a sense of the language of fishing, and it soon becomes apparent that the language which fishermen have used to describe their hopes and disconsolations also encodes the ways in which people have thought about the pastime.

In the earliest English records there is no mention of rod-and-line fishing. Fish there are in abundance – Bede, writing in c.700, explicitly states that British waters teem with salmon, eels, and pike – but there are no angle-rods, no casting, none of fishing's refinements. This pattern continues into the late Old English period: in Aelfric's *Dialogues*, written at the turn of the 10th century and intended for boys studying Latin, mention is made of a fisherman (indeed, other dialogues include a huntsman and a fowler), and again of abundance of fish, since the fisherman is 'unable to catch as many as I can sell', but these fish are surely taken either on nets or on set-lines. Nor was it likely that in this period of English history there would be many or any who would have the leisure to fish as a 'disport'; the energy of the time is the energy of courage and fear, rather than the energy of enjoyment as a later age would come to know the term. And what Englishman would tie flies when the prows of Eirik's warships nosed up the Humber? Here, though, the lexical bedrock of fishing vocabulary is laid down: terms like *angle, beetle, creeper, drag, fish, gnat, hook, midge, wade* and so on are all pre-Conquest. The natural world is being descriptively appropriated.

Then comes the greatest of cultural disasters, the Norman Conquest. In its wake, the language is inundated with French loan-words, or Latin words transmitted via French. Simultaneously, one has the first, albeit belated, lexical inheritance from the Scandinavian settlers of two and three centuries before; these are again non-piscatorial, words such as (arguably) *grilse, mort, voe*. From Old French, or from Latin via French, come the words *blank, brace, cane, fry, mend, salmon, spawn, troll* (from *troller,* 'to quest') and several others. And if the language is recognisable, it is surely no accident that it is at this medieval stage that fishing literature begins in earnest, with the *Treatise*, in a mid 15th century text, later gathered into the *Book of St. Albans* by England's first publishing entrepreneur, Wynkyn de Worde.

As the centuries pass, more Latin words are borrowed into English (the borrowing reflecting the relative status of the two languages), and description becomes ever more refined: *action, antenna, barb, caudal, chironomid, diptera, dorsal, eclosion.* . . . There are words of discrimination and detail, words of scholarship endorsed by time and use. And of course, as the 16th century passes into the 17th and 18th, fishing literature spawns endlessly: Mascall poaches the *Treatise*; Walton poaches Mascall (particularly the list of flies); Cotton is typically energetic and first-handed, as is Venables; and then to Chetham, and Bowlker, and Scotcher, and Stewart; and beyond; and to us.

There are two things discernible as time pours into the future: one is that the language of fishing gives us a vital clue as to the history and structure of the 'disport'. As the first records begin, fishing is a matter of utility, a matter of resource and food. I think it is safe to infer from this that, at least in England, there was no rod and line fishing much before Magna Carta. For the native inhabitants it would have been unlikely, even if monks did keep fish ponds; for the Scandinavian settlers I find it implausible. Even abstracting from the erroneous image of rape and pillage, their manners would more likely run to husbandry than hunting, or perhaps a stone in the fist, a hand under the bank, a gaff in a gill. For the aristocrats newly come from France, however – their original Viking manners barely disguised under a thin glaze of civilisation – it would have been possible for rod and line fishing to have taken place. They, and they alone, had the leisure to fish, to hawk and to hunt game in their far-flung estates (although hawking was also a pastime of the English nobility late in the Anglo-Saxon period). And it cannot be coincidental that just as the medieval vocabulary of fishing draws on the legacy of French, so English fishing literature is, as John Waller Hills claimed, deeply moulded and conditioned by French writings. By the Middle Ages, for example, the rose-moles all in stipple, once described inelegantly as belonging to a *sceote*, an Old English 'shoat', now belong to the trout, 'a right choice fish and also a fervent biter'. *Trout* is originally

Latin (*tructus*; this would also give rise to a variant in *truff*); the adjectives used to describe it, choice and fervent, enter the language from France in the 13th century. Fishing is coming of age: hunger gives way to sportsmanship.

The second thing that emerges from a study of fly-fishing's language is the intensity and delight – delight, again – with which fishermen have described their quarry. Many examples could be found, all testifying to the vivid relationship between hunter and hunted, but I will here focus on just one set of words, the words used to describe the sea trout.

Of all game fish, the sea trout seems to have most names. The ones in more or less common use include *finnock, herling, mort, peal, scurf, sewin, smelt, sprod, truff, white trout,* and *whitling*. In addition, the Oxford English Dictionary lists many other local or specialised terms: *bull trout, forktail, grey trout, harvest cock, herring peal, may peal, pugg peal, salmon trout* and *yellowfin*. That yields twenty terms; include the normative *sea trout*, and that gives us the sea trout's twenty-first birthday, its adult lexical distribution.

The plethora of terms can be interpreted in significant ways. In one sense it seems to be the case that the sea trout was recognised as a sporting fish in its own right only belatedly. The term *sea trout* is first attested in 1745, very late, and it is perhaps only in the 19th century that the sea trout gains a well-defined place in the sporting hierarchy. Francis Francis, for example, writing in 1875, wrote 'Next to the salmon ranks in value for sport the sea trout. Of these there are two kinds . . .' And of course Grey devotes a whole chapter of his great *Fly-fishing* (1899) to the sea trout. The fact that the sea trout is only clearly recognised as a sporting proposition in the 19th century is, as an incidental point, not unconnected with the development of railways, which gave sporting anglers access to Scotland (and parts of Ireland), where they and their families could enjoy a summer escape shooting, and fishing for salmon and their cousins, sea trout.

In earlier times, though, the profusion of terms indicates uncertainty as to what the fish actually was. If *mort* is taken to derive from Old Norse *mergð* *('great, big')*, then it is our oldest word for the sea trout. On the other hand, one would expect a Norse antonym to exist concurrently, and this does not appear to have been recorded. It is possible that for many centuries the sea trout was mistaken for either a trout, or (in its largest incarnations) as a salmon; the *Treatise* makes no mention of it as a separate species, and Walton does not speak of sea trout but does mention the 'Fordidge trout . . . [which] . . . knows his times . . . of coming into that river out of the sea, where he lives, and, it is like, feeds nine months of the year . . .' It seems, however, that there must have been confused recognition of the fish as a distinct species by this time, since many sea trout words are first attested in the 16th century: *peal*, possibly from Old French *palle*, 'of a whitish appearance'; *sewin* (etymology unknown); *whitling* (1597, from white + the diminutive suffix, -ling). And here too are the first hints of fascination with the fish's appearance, specifically, its whiteness, its blue-whiteness fresh off the tide. Later, and from Gaelic, this theme is picked up in the word *finnock*, first attested in 1771, from the Gaelic root *fionn*, 'white', and the Anglo-Irish (now uniquely Irish) term *white trout*. In the 19th century, as taxonomy ran riot, the same fish is classified as *Salmo albus*, white salmonid. Even the word *herling*, whose ultimate etymology is unknown, may pick up the same theme if it is distantly related to *herring* (as in the local term *herring peal*). So think, as you admire two brace of sea trout on the bow thwart one evening and see the sun begin to set on their tight-scaled, silver cleanness, that others, many and greater, have also watched like you, and, like you, have turned for home with white scales on their hands. The absorption with the hunted is also inscribed in fishing's language: it is the adoration of the trout.

But perhaps, after all, there are too many words: *of making many books there is no end; and much study is a weariness of the flesh.*

Although, when the first words of this book were written, I had little idea of where their meaning would take me, I knew beyond all words that somehow and somewhere in the years by lakes and rivers – by the becks, by the expensive stillwaters, by sea trout rivers at night and by the rock-littered beaches of the west, by grayling streams, the brawl of occasional salmon runs and the bay of the Black Dog – somehow I had begun to miss what fishing in the first place brought to me. It would be too easy to dismiss this as mere nostalgia, too dramatic to claim it was a desertion by delight. Rather, it was a sense of disquiet, the kind of dereliction brought by an absence of principle and by obscured purposes. Sometimes, after all, it is both wise and necessary to mount a cogent moral defence of one's own exhausted happiness, since in making that defence one may find happiness afresh. Having come this far, then, far enough beyond principles and landscapes and the faces gone gently into the dark, beyond waste and witness, it is time to come to the sense of an ending, or perhaps, a new beginning. And so, where our paths diverge and lead to different waters, I will say this:

If we have been gifted at all, it is the shadowlands of time past and their waterside ghosts who have bequeathed us our present and equipped us with some sort of hope for, and trust in the future. Change there always is, but there is also continuity; there is loss, but there is also augmentation; there is the silent mental shuffle of worry, but there is also the vividness of experiment and the absorption of Aprils; there is doubt, but there is also promise.

And after all that, here is yesterday, lying open at a page which is, as was promised, 'principally for your solace'; here too is tomorrow, implied in all you say and do and read, modified by the present; and here am I, becoming fictional, hurrying slowly to go fishing again, down through the fields and the forked path through the darkening trees, haunted by the boy catching minnows in Harden beck who dreamed these moments out of happiness and puzzle. And thirty years on, as I vanish into an evening tempted by the suck and heavy swirl of rising trout, I know also and finally that for him, and for me, and for our ancestors' ancestors, the word *dream* meant 'joy'.

CHAPTER NINE
The Haunted Country

*H*e stood on the old road bridge in the midsummer darkness. The warmth of the early midnight – midges, the soft clumsiness of moths, and bats invisibly jagging the last light of the sky – had given way to the damp chill of the hours before dawn. The river, too low for fishing, flowed itself to sleep over the cooling rocks.

'What we need,' John Joyce had said to him yesterday, 'is a tondershore.' But no thundershower had come, and the weather remained calm and the glass in the cottage high. The days passed with sailing, or listless sunbathing and ice-creams followed by murderous cocktails and cheap novels. The nights came in with a walk down to the hopeless river. There had been no fish on the hotel slab for two weeks, and bookings had been cancelled. The bars were almost silent. The air was pent with a storm which would not break.

The river, louder under the bridge, dreamed of the sea's high interiors, and rain. The sea trout came in to the river mouths with each tide, and out again on the ebb, back fins awash; the sea trout were turning black in the salt water. The only fish in the river were the ones that had run three weeks before, a small group of big trout that John had watched over the stones down at Inverkyle, the harbingers of the main July shoals. 'Big fellas,' John had said, and then, as an afterthought over the last of the hipflasks, 'big as farmyard beasts'. John was a good old man – drunken, certainly, and inaccurate, perhaps, but his hand lacked no cunning with rod and line. If he knew every sea trout lie between Inverkyle and Lamish it was because he had fished where he had poached, and he had poached under the bridge. Those narrows were poached still: two hundredweight rocks on either side of the river told where the net had been stretched. By this month in a normal season, the Bridge Pool would hold hundreds of trout. Now, in unnatural times, it held perhaps six fish, trout that spent each day in the deep water, concentrating on breathing, secretive and elusive. At night, equally elusive, one or two of them would thrash in the shrunken stream, drought-stricken, fraught with a meaningless energy.

The clear mountains were swept by infrequent cloud and constant stars. He told the names to himself: Ben Quaich, Ben Strighdh, Ben Fuar, Ben Duimh . . . and eight more. The Circle of the Twelve: haunted country. Years before, his clever, well-paid and talented friend, then a journalist with the *Frankfurter Allgemeine* and expert on European Communism (a born sceptic) had accepted a bet to spend the night alone on the shoulder of Ben Strighdh. They had waved him off after closing-time from the back bar of the Lamish Hotel. He had gone up the hill singing. Three days later, after a rescue search, they had found him. He was still singing – a misty, curious music. He was never the same. Now, infested and in rags, he pushed a pram up the roads of the west coast, and waved vacantly to everyone, or burbled God. His lips were coated in spittle, and he seemed happy.

There was also the story of the Viking gold. Two

Edinburgh students on an afternoon excursion had found a cave in low cloud on the skirts of Ben Duimh hard by the sea. Sheltering, they had explored. The cave led them into the mountain yard by yard. At the bottom of the shaft, by puny torch-light, they had found a Viking ship, and sleeping warriors covered in gold trappings – armour, armlets, corslets, small shields and spear-tips. Returning after two hours to the cave mouth, they had taken a compass fix and half-walked, half-run the six miles back to their rented house. The newspapers in the living room were dated two days after the afternoon they had left for Ben Duimh. An air and sea search had been mounted for them. They could never find the cave again. They, too, had been his friends.

He pulled on his jacket against the cold, and poured a stiff shot of whisky. A dog barked in the distance, and on the horizon the light from Missen Head threw out a regular arc under a weak moon. But the sea was calm tonight, a melancholy, long, withdrawing roar.

He lit a cigarette and drew in a lungful of French tobacco smoke mixed with thin night air. He swallowed whisky. Then mechanically he picked up the rod from where it rested against the stone parapet, unhooked the fly from the keeper ring and ran his fingers along the leader, checking for wind-knots. The tackle was good. The rod had cost a great deal of money. He had told himself he deserved it after being sent his first royalty cheque. He loved the rod. Every winter since, he had rubbed it down with fine emery paper, and revarnished it so that it was non-reflecting and matt. He had picked stray fish-scales off the surface of the carbon with a pair of tweezers and taken a toothbrush to the mud ingrained in the struts of the butt ring. It passed the time, the long, fishingless evenings of December. He looked after the reel, all his reels, with the same absorption. He was a priest attending the details of his faith.

His hand felt the dwindling of the tapered leader, expected, and got, the sting of the barb. He paused, took out a small torch from his pocket, and shielding the beam from the water, directed the point of light towards the fly. The Leander Blue: his own fly, tied when his mind was running with alcohol and sea trout, and named after a race horse which he'd believed in but lost money on. Eventually he had abandoned hope, refused to back the horse at any price. Next time out, it came in at 20:1. He didn't credit serendipity. Leander Blue was an apt name for a fly.

It was an experimental pattern, but unlike most experiments of the kind, it had worked. He had made it for this river. He had thought of it being fished across the pool downstream, a blue-black and tinsel fragment. He thought of the fish rising to meet it, clean-scaled and curious. He thought of the line drawing away into the darkness, and the rod arching up, and the sudden weight of silence that follows.

The fly was tied on a low-water salmon iron. He had fashioned the body from wide silver Mylar, and ribbed it for strength with finer wire. For the wing, he had tied in strands of black bucktail, overlaid with some strands of light mallard or teal to relieve the sombre effect. The hackle was bearded, a few fibres of black hen teased in with some blue jay. Finally, he had added some junglecock cheeks; they made the fly look finished, and reminded him of the old salmon patterns he'd seen in Owen's wallet. He had imagined the fly in the peat water, the silhouette of it, the gleams of it. He had decided it must work. And it had.

But tonight it could not work. The river was too low, the fish too few, or too lethargic, even to follow it. He had fished for an hour before midnight, careful cast over cast into the best water. He had felt the line slacken each time as it passed out of the current, and each time he had increased the speed of the retrieve. His fly was a small fish, darting into the stiller water at his side of the pool. But apart from one moving trout at the pool head, he had seen nothing, and felt nothing in his hands but the drag of the stream.

He sat on a rock and drank more whisky. Then he bit off the fly from the leader and let the end of the nylon dangle from his thumb and index finger. It was colder. He was glad he'd brought the waistcoat and the extra sweater. He looked at the battered bicycle beside him; its dull metal caught the pallor of the empty eastern sky. He heard a car take the turn for Inverkyle two miles away – holiday folk driving late and unsteadily home from Fergie's Bar at Altnabreac. Fresh scampi and chips in a basket, unused fishing tackle in the back of a Jaguar. They would buy a salmon from John Joyce's freezer to take back, and would say they'd had a wonderful time, the weather had been fantastic.

He thought of clouds massing in the mid-Atlantic, and sodden light, and a gale from the west, and three days and nights of rain, the isobars packed tight round Iceland. And he thought of the thousands of sea trout waiting in the estuary to run, and the miles of nylon nets they had passed, the bladderwrack, the kelp, the salmon-farms and hulls of boats, to return to this river and the pools in which they were spawned. Even then, even so, there were the seals; more nets; gaffs; poison; and fishermen. But every year, somehow, the fish got through, rested in the same lies, and cut their redds in the same places every autumn, in remote trickles out in the bog where there was only moss, water, and the wind.

They had left a light on at the cottage, so the turf fire would still be warm. He liked turf smoke. After a fortnight, his sweaters would smell of it, an essence of the west he took back south along with a piece of bog-cotton, a spray of heather, and the photographs. He had thought of burning turf at home, but it would have seemed out of place there. He looked again at the bicycle. His back was stiff. It was eight miles to ride, past cows coughing on poor pasture, and past malevolent dogs that ran at him from gateways, their eyes glinting. Then downhill to the coast road, freewheeling by White Island towards the hump of Carn Mountain and the cottage light.

A fish lunged out of the darkness ten yards way, a shocking thump of a splash like a half-brick dropped carelessly from the sky. Instantly he was fully awake. John Joyce had told him there was was a fish lying in the thin water at the head of the pool; it must have been the same fish he had heard move earlier. Maybe it was a restless sea trout, one of the big fish which had run three weeks ago, confined now to a patch of water in the draw of current beside an abutting rock. Or perhaps it was an early salmon, turning coloured in the same place, waiting for autumn, its jaw kyping and its body wasting away until it held just the curds of milt. But he was sure it was a trout. The rock was a good lie for a trout, and he'd taken other fish there.

He lit another cigarette and began to think. Catching the fish was unlikely, but he might move it. If he moved it, he would come back tomorrow when there was more warmth and less light from the burnt moon and fish it again. With this low water, the trout wouldn't stray far, not as far, he thought, as the Butts. He caught the end of the leader again, and turned on the torch. He opened the flybox. He had already decided that conventional patterns would not work for this fish, although it was hard to tell how or why he'd taken the decision. The smoke from the cigarette stung his eyes. He imagined the fish quiet, its gills hardly moving, under the water by the rock. Why do sea trout leap? He dismissed the question as an irrelevance, but immediately he had a vivid pan-image of a sea trout he had once risen to the dap on Loch Shiel. It had chased the skating fly for two yards across the entrance to Coul Bay, and then, as the fly lifted, it had leaped, a burnished blue plume of sheer fish. Sea trout chase the dap because it is trying to escape, because they see the wake, because they harry baitfish in the sea that way . . .

Shiel and the dap. The sea trout by the stone. Gradually, connections began to half-form in his mind, but seemed to make no sense. He thought more solidly of the text-book wisdom: sea trout, when they have been some time in the river, will often accept smaller patterns of trout fly. This was true. Away on the east coast years before, he had watched a sea trout for three months during the summer. After the first month, he had seen the white of its mouth underwater during a large evening hatch of fly. It turned, like a brown trout, after ascending nymphs. It may not have been feeding, but it certainly remembered feeding, and maybe it was trying to feed. '. . . will often accept . . .' The skating dap. A sea trout leaping.

On the last leaf of the flybox he saw some patterns tied up for stillwater trout, big Muddlers with clipped deer-hair heads and gold tinsel bodies. Phrases from the fishing journals pricked his mind: our old friend, *Cottus gobio*, the bullhead; or the Cockatush minnow; or a monstrous, malformed sedge. Greased, the Muddler would float and cause a wake. He saw the V of the wake by the sea trout rock, and already he felt the fish stir after the swimming thing. He took out the biggest of the lures and knotted it on, six turns and the Half-Blood well tucked. The leader tippet was six pounds test. Then he dunked the fly into the bottle of floatant. He clicked off the torch, picked up the bag, and let his eyes accustom with the night. *But I have promises to keep/ And miles to go before I sleep.'* Robert Frost sang inconsequently into his head. He dropped down from the road, his feet scuffing stems in the turf, and walked slowly towards the stones at the head of the pool.

It was a difficult cast. The bank was high behind him and behind the bank was the massive stonework of the bridge. The fly could catch on the backcast, or hit the stone, breaking off the barb or even the bend of the lure. The fish had moved eight yards out into the current, hard into the far side of the rock whose black shadow he saw in the paler stream. The problem was to get a clean cast out into the neck of the pool and then to fish the lure so that it swung waking across the glide by the rock. The lure could not be allowed to fish too far across into the near bank, or else it would snag. He tucked the rod under his right arm, caught the leader with his left hand, and blew on the fly to dry it, to work the floatant in. Perhaps it would be better to fish from downstream, and cast up. But then the lure would fish at the same speed as the current, unless he retrieved it fiercely, and it wouldn't drag to cause a wake. It was better to cast from where he stood upstream of the rock.

He waded out again into the dark water. Above Ben Duimh, the moon was gradually hindered by cloud. He let the fly fall from his left hand, and, pulling some loops of line from the reel, got the fly-line working outside the rod-tip. He pulled some more line from the reel and shot it all at the next cast, keeping his wrist stiff and his arm high on the upstroke so that the fly would clear the bank behind his back. The steeple cast. He'd learned it from pictures in a book. He felt the line snake out across the river. The current took the line and swung it round to his left. The fly would be skating across the neck, reaching the rock. Instinctively he raised the rod, at the same time drawing line with his left hand to make the lure swim upstream so it would not snag. The line came back to him easily. Rolling out a loop of line, he cast again. The lure swished in the air. The fish had moved ten minutes ago. They took the floating lure with an enormous purpose, although sometimes they were impossible to hook, nipping the fibres with an incongruous delicacy. He reminded himself that just to raise the fish would be an achievement.

The line fished round below him. The greased Muddler dragged unseen across the low water. He pulled in some line with his left hand and raised the rod to keep the fly clear of the rock. He pulled off another yard of line, and cast at a steeper angle towards the shadows. The fly would now be falling within a foot or two of the far bank, near the poaching stone. He fished it back towards him silently, grey as thought, slipping the ripple. He judged again from the weight of the line and elapsed time that the Muddler would be covering the fish. Again he pulled line with his left hand, and raised the rod, swinging it to his right. He was too late. Even as the rod went over he felt the solidity of the line, and knew the lure had caught the far side of the rock. He kept the line taut for a moment. He would roll-cast downstream, and try to free the fly with the momentum of the new cast and a different angle. He lowered the rod.

Instead of the line slackening as he expected, the pressure was maintained. The rod bent more firmly into the night, and more, and he felt the pressure of the line in his left hand. The line was live and the rod suddenly kicked. By instinct he caught the spare loop between his thumb and index finger, close to the corks, and raised the rod towards the stars, letting any slack run out on tension through the rings. He felt the weight of the fish slew sideways, beyond the rock in the neck of the pool, and heard a dull, boiling thrash break the murmur of the stream. He wondered how he'd hooked the sea trout, since he had felt nothing but the rock. But the sea trout was the rock, living. The thought came to him that he would never get this fish.

As if in response, the sea trout ran, not downstream as he had expected, but upstream, under the arch of the bridge and into the deeper blackness towards the Butts. The reel frailed on its check and he felt the carbon-fibre move under the corks in his right hand. Towards the point, sixty yards away, he heard a fish leap, disembodied. The power surged back down the line and into his arm. The fish kept running, the muscles in its body a constant flex against the downstream pressure. He knew that this was dangerous, that the fish would leap again somewhere at the end of its run, an invisible charge of arched back and stiffened fins, but he kept the rod high and the line unslackened. His body shook. Once he had been hit by a car, and his body had shaken like this and he had wet himself uncontrollably. He clenched his mind against itself.

Eighty yards away, the sea trout plunged. The rod came back weightless and the line sagged into the shallows at his feet. He realised that the fish had turned somewhere off Green Point. He wound clumsily, hoping the line would reel onto the spool without trapping or coiling, because there would be another run and the line would need to pay out freely. There were weed beds between the bridge and Green Point. If the fish were clever, it would swim into the thickest clump of strands, and the fight would be over because he could not follow the fish upstream along the bank. He had to work the fish back into the pool below him. He kept reeling, feeling droplets of river water spray off the spindle and the back of the spool, holding the rod high. There was always the possibility that the fish had shed the hook at the end of its first run.

He had not reeled fast enough and the line, bellied in the black current, had circled below him, caught by the river. Then his hands weighed again, and he knew the fish was still connected, downstream this time. It had covered eighty, nearly a hundred, yards of current in about twelve seconds, but still ran, down towards the Slate, and further, down towards the Flat Stones on the far bank where the Croaghnadubh meets the main river. He felt the power of the fish in his hands. He swung the rod to his left, trying uselessly to side-strain the fish so that it would not run the Croagh, the hill stream. Again, disastrously, the rod went slack. A bat nittered under the bridge, close to his head. He felt his flesh crawl, and the dead limpness of the line in his left hand. The moon emerged from behind the high cloud, and rode into the stars. The river silvered in the pool; the symmetry of Orion disciplined the sky.

He wound again, expecting nothing. The backward taper of the fly-line came back onto the spool. Then, twenty yards out, another solid resistance, though different from the first wild rushes. A series of massive shocks went down to the rod butt, a series of scaled pulses that felt as if the leader were being beaten with bags of cement. He realised slowly that the fish had turned again at the Croagh mouth, and had swum back towards him intent, its head down. Now the great fish was shaking its head against the barb and the pressure, and flailing at the line with its tail. He absorbed each wrench with his whole body, gave line, took line, a foot at a time. His arm began to ache dully, and he tucked the reel-seat and rod butt against his right wrist for leverage. The fish, deep in the current, continued to flail, coming closer. Then it ran straight towards him and turned a massive flank three feet from his waders. He was drenched with water and phosphorescence. The fish swam away, quieter now, upstream again. He thought of the six-pound tippet, and of the hookhold. A hookhold in a fish this size could be a precarious thing. The scissors were the best place. He imagined the Muddler over the barb, deep in the fish's maxillary. He thought again of the great fish, knowing that he would never fight a better fish than this.

The fish had stopped. He still felt the weight on the rod and in his hands, but the weight was a constant thing. He kept the rod up and bent, and occasionally felt the action pull away, as if the fish was twisting its body around a pillar. It was hard to know what had happened, but he guessed that the fish had run into one of the big weed beds below Green Point and lay there, swaying and flexing between the stems, a weight he couldn't move by force alone. Perhaps the nylon leader had twisted round the very base of the weeds. If he couldn't move the fish, the fight was over. But this fish was the best he had ever played, and he wanted to beat it although he didn't think he could. For the moment, at least, there was nothing he could do. It was three o'clock in the morning. The eastern sky lightened over Ben Fuar.

The sea trout was fast, and there would be little danger if he put down the rod for a moment. He poured another large shot of whisky into the metal cup of the flask and lit another cigarette. He could not follow the fish upstream because the water was too deep to wade under the bridge, too difficult to swim in the dark. Therefore he would not be able to work the fish out by rod pressure. He would have to get the great fish to help him.

He drained the whisky. Then he slipped the bag off his shoulders and unclipped the landing-net from the D-ring.

He walked up to the road, carrying the net, unsliding the telescopic ferrule as he went, then locking the handle so that it was at its fullest extension. He climbed across the barbed wire into Cummins' unkept field, and crossed the dew-fallen land until he reached the river again a hundred yards below Green Point. 'Alright, fish,' he said aloud, and the air took his words away, mocking him.

By the first lightening of the sky he began to make out the far bank of the river. He began to make out the weed beds. He walked cautiously into the river below where he thought the fish was fast, pushing out the handle of the net in front of him. He would wade as far across the river as he could, using the handle of the net to find the fly-line trailing back from the fish's mouth. The river was deeper here, its bed stone and silt, where the weeds rooted. He felt the quiet current drag powerfully against his legs. He waded further, probing for the line. He had to move slowly and with care. If he scared the fish by a sudden pull, a clumsy mistake with the net handle, the fish might run past him downstream. The line would then be looped absurdly round his waders, and the leader would break. The current grew stronger. He imagined the fish recovering its strength in it, all the power coming back to its body now the draw from the rod was off.

Just over halfway across the river, he found the fly-line. Gingerly he raised the line from the water surface with the handle of the net, and brought it towards his hand. This was a dangerous manoeuvre. He didn't want to let the fish feel what he was doing. Very carefully he began to wade upstream, inch by inch, tracing the line into the weeds. It took him ten minutes until he saw the line angled down from his hand into a trailing bed. The fish was in there somewhere, breathing, strengthening. He let go of the line and backed quietly out of the river. On the bank again, he stretched, resting his back and arms, riving out the knots in his muscles. It was early morning, and almost full light. An unknown bird tried a song from the telegraph pole at the bridge, then stopped. The washed, unwoken world. He tasted a breeze on his face, carrying the sea.

He waded back in to the river above the weed bed, holding the handle of the net out in front of him, pointing downstream. He wanted to goad the fish out, to send it running down into the Bridge Pool. He knew the ploy was too simple, that it might well not work. The fish could easily break the leader. It could easily bury itself deeper in the weed, or simply run into another impossible place.

He prodded the fronds that spread below him. He saw clearly how the leader anchored into the offside of the clump, the fly-line trailing below it. He wondered whether the hook still held, or whether the fish had gone, leaving the hook immovably in the toughest stems. He prodded again, sweeping the net handle back and forth through the fronds, searching. Under his eyes the weed bed began to shake unnaturally, and he saw for the first time the great flank of the fish arching away from the handle of the net, two feet and more of gunmetal grey, and the white leading edges of the pectoral fins. Then the torsion of the fish's body displaced silt from the river-bed, and a few shorn strands of weed floated away. The fish was trying to rub the leader across the weed stems. He imagined the taut leader sawing through. He had to save this situation, and quickly. 'You can't frighten me, fish,' he said, although the fish could, and knew it. He waded directly towards the fish, wanting to scare it out into the current. He waved his arms and yelled. He beat the water with the flat of his hand. As he bent, the river tipped into the back of his waders.

Then he saw the line doubling back, the peach tip turning downstream and moving away, and he knew that he had scared the fish out into more open water. Even if it had run into another weed bed, the hold would not be so firm. He didn't wait to see where the line went, but moved quickly out of the water, pushing up bow waves from his legs, and squelched up the bank, running heavily and slowly towards the bridge and his abandoned rod. Already his feet felt wet and raw; his arms and back still ached from the fight after midnight; and he was cold again. But he began to realise that he was going to fight this fish to the end.

He reached the place where he had left the rod. The line trailed into the belly of the pool, its taper partly sunk. For once, the great fish had made a mistake. It was tired and confused. It had regained no strength in the weed bed because lying in the current had taken energy it could not afford to lose. He reeled in the loose line, his hands wet. He felt the rod connect directly with the fish, and pull over to meet the weight. The fish swam towards him again, deep, shaking its head among the stones on the bottom of the pool. He held it on a steady length of line as it began to swim round. He imagined its jaws opening and closing underwater, trying to shake out the hook, gulping oxygen from the stream. He kept it on the steady length of line, feeling it pulse. He reached for a cigarette with his left hand, wary in case the fish made a sudden run. But he knew the fish had little strength left to run, perhaps one more rush when it saw the net. He lit the cigarette, trapping the line between his fingers. The sea breeze carried the smoke away. He would have liked whisky and hot, fresh coffee.

The great fish was close to him now, closer to the surface, weakening, always under pressure. It cruised ten yards away across the stream, and he saw the massive square tail circle once then disappear. 'I am going to beat you, fish,' he thought. He reached behind himself for the net, which he had left propped against the bank.

The net was big enough for sea trout. He had even landed two salmon in the same net last season. But as he placed the net in the water in front of him, he knew that this fish was too big. It was unnatural; it would wreck the metal bow with one lash of its body. The bigger salmon net was back at the cottage. He could not tail the fish; sea trout will not be tailed, the wrist above the caudal fin is too narrow and the fin itself collapses.

Suddenly the fish came right to the surface, and crushed the current violently with its tail – once, twice, three times. It was trying to smash the leader on the top of the pool, against the tight line. It lashed its tail again, and this time he felt the jolt deep in the rod. The fish rolled twice in coils of water, and then disappeared. The water darkened around its body. He felt the fish sound. The breeze began to hiss on the taper. The eastern sky was ominously red.

He still had no plan to land the fish. He had a dim idea that the best ways would be either to beach it, or gill it. The first was risky, and depended on the hookhold; the second was almost impossible because of the writhing weight of the fish's body in his hands. He worked the fish towards the surface, hooping the rod, taking line onto the reel. He saw the junction of the fly-line and the leader, and heard the different note of the wind catching the nylon, a shriller pitch. The great fish came up, working its jaws, its inside mouth a vivid white in the wine-red river. As it reached the surface, it cartwheeled. He saw the whole length and bulk of the sea trout for the first time, and heard the water crack apart as its flank ripped back into the river. 'You are beaten, fish,' he said.

The sea trout began to wallow six yards out, trying to pull its head down into the current, turning, and tensing again. Now he had control over the fish, and the fish could not fight the rod nor the river any more. He angled the rod to allow the fish upstream of him. He would work the fish into the stones at his feet, pulling it off balance, waiting until it turned on its side and then maintaining the pressure so that the fish beached itself.

Heavy and strengthless, the fish came on to him under the arch of the bridge. He backed away up the bank, keeping the rod high. He watched the fish turn onto its flank and the current brought it towards the stones. He saw the hook, clicked into the bone and skin above the maxillary. It was a good hookhold, the fly in down to the bend. The fish came onto the stones, turned, churning the water, and the rod bucked. He gave line as the sea trout regained the deeper water. He would have to try again.

He angled the rod out over the neck of the pool, moving the fish under pressure towards the bridge. He didn't want the fish below him in the current. He backed up the bank again, and the fish, still feebly lashing its tail, turned onto its side, grey and white, black swastika spots above its lateral line. This time he kept on the pressure as the fish touched the stones. The fish writhed, its own bulk driving it further into the shallow water, further towards the bank. He kept everything solid, reeling in the line he had gained. He saw that the great fish was beached on the stones, that the fight was over and that he had beaten the best fish he was ever likely to see.

He kept the rod up and the line taut, and walked carefully down to where the fish lay, its gills working haphazardly. He transferred the rod to his left hand and bent down, hooking the fingers of his right hand directly under the fish's gill cover. The fish was almost too heavy to lift with one hand; instead, he slid the fish up the bank, onto the wet grass, feeling the very last of its strength working against his arm. He lay it in the hollow by his bag. He had never seen a bigger sea trout; its body was as thick as his thigh. His arms ached.

He fetched the priest from the outside pocket of his bag and knelt by the fish, pressing the palm of his left hand against the flank to control it. Then he used both hands to turn the fish upright, so that he could make a clean strike with the priest. He held the fish's body against the top of his waders, and made three blows with the lead-bored wood. The fish quivered gently, its fins shuddering beyond the instant of death. Then it was still.

He left the fish in the hollow, took the Thermos from the bag, and sat two yards away on the smooth, wet grass. He poured coffee, cold and bitter. His hands shook. He reached inside his coat for the hipflask, and drank the rest of the whisky in one shot. Then he zipped up his jacket, and hugged his arms round his chest, getting the circulation going by slapping his hands. The sun was almost up.

He went back to the great fish to unhook the fly. The Muddler was almost stripped bare of dressing. That was the fish, rubbing the lure into the bottom of the weed bed in the early hours of the morning. Gently he prised open the fish's jaw for a better purchase on the shank of the hook. He wondered how long the fish had been at sea, whether this was its third or fourth spawning run. Later he would take scales from under the fish's dorsal fin, and send them away to be analysed.

There was blood in the mouth of the fish near the fly. The barb was in deep, and he lifted the open mouth towards his face to see where his fingers could work best. His fingers slid with blood and mucous from the fish's body. He looked into the open mouth and grasped the shank of the hook, prising it out, with three sharp twists, from the gristle in the jaw. As the hook came free, he saw something glint in the blood at the back of the fish's throat, behind the vomer. He pushed his index finger into the fish's throat, and felt metal. He levered the thing out, puzzled, and placed it on the fish's dorsal flank. Then he took the piece of towel he always kept in his pocket, and wet it at the edge of the river. He wiped the blood away from the fish's gills and jaw, and the mud from the fish's tail. He picked up the small metal and rubbed it carefully across the damp cloth. He folded the dry piece of the towel over the metal. He opened the folds. On the palm of his hand was a gold ring.

He turned to face the flaming light in the eastern sky, bending to look at the clear circle of twisted gold. A small ring. For safety, he tried it on the fourth finger of his right hand, then on his little finger, where it pushed smoothly across the mid-joint. He held up his hand to the east. The sun rose behind the shoulder of Ben Fuar and the light struck the ring in front of his eyes, the slim circle an unmarked radiance.

He lowered his hand, and looked round in the teeming light to the hollow where he had tended and left the great fish. A sheep cropped loudly. The grass was straight, short, and undisturbed. The fish he had fought for hours, the great, impossible and perfect fish, was gone.

He fingered the gold on his right hand, and frowned a little. He went back to the rod and hooked the stripped Muddler back into the keeper ring. Elsewhere, the gross world began to wake and go about its business. Bird-song would fill the suburban avenues, and there would be the quiet electricity of milk-floats on their rounds. Polluted tide would succeed polluted tide, and computer would hum to computer across the wide spaces of money and need. The joggers, the incomers and the fanatic would pant round the parks before breakfast and a shower, and the city would gather itself in durance. Pigeons would preen in the sun, the desert would creep over Africa and Brazil, and the met-alled, unentire and forsaken planet would spin in the heat.

He sat on, and watched the sun rise in a red flood of cloud over Ben Fuar. The twisted circle burnt his finger with a cold flame. The sun, the wind and cloud cast moving shadows on the land. The storm would break. Today it would rain. The sun cleared Ben Fuar. He could smell the sea. Aching with fatigue and loss, he told himself again the stories of the haunted country, and the story of the great fish. They had already become history, the figures of a dark fiction. And, of course, it was better so.